2

first steps

first steps

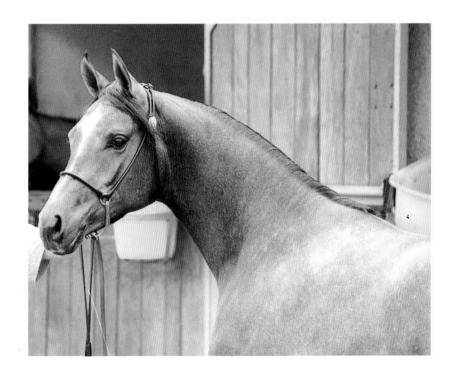

Jane van Lennep

J. A. Allen
London

British Library Cataloguing in Publication Data
A catalogue record for this book is available
from the British Library.

ISBN 0.85131.619.0

Published in Great Britain in 1995 by
J. A. Allen & Company Limited
1 Lower Grosvenor Place, London SW1W 0EL

Designed by Nancy Lawrence
Text editor Elizabeth O'Beirne-Ranelagh

Typeset in Hong Kong by
Setrite Typesetters Ltd.
Printed in Spain by Printeksa S.A.
Colour processing by Tenon & Polert Colour
Scanning Ltd, Hong Kong

Thanks to the following for permission to use the
photographs on the pages indicated: Nancy Aiston vi,
viii, xi, 4 (top), 24, 25, 26, 41, 46 (base right), 53, 55,
60, 67 (top), 74, 76, (centre, bottom), 79, 97, 146,
151; Dengie Crops Ltd 106; Pat Dyke 63; Equestrian
Services Thorney 73 (top); Alex Fell 82; Lorna
Freeman 72 (top); Bob Langrish ii, vii, xiii, 10, 172;
David van Lennep 44, 45, 46 (except base right), 48,
49, 56, 72 (bottom), 112, 133; June van Lennep 58;
Elizabeth O'Beirne-Ranelagh 61; Neil Roberts xiv, 18
(top); Caroline Searle 103 (top); Jackie Shanks 183.
All other photographs were taken by the author.

Frontispiece: Youngstock at Welton Stud.
Title page: Arab filly at Al Waha Stud.
Previous page (left and right): Young Arabs at
Heronstream Stud.
Right: The author visits a two-year-old filly at grass
in late summer.
Far right: Young Thoroughbreds at the Oaks.

CONTENTS

Foreword by Julie Kibble   *page* ix
Preface   xi
Acknowledgements   xiii

1   Introduction: pros and cons   1
2   Acquiring a young horse   3
3   A safe home   11
4   Lessons for the first year: now catch your horse   21
5   Further first year lessons: tying and grooming   29
6   Into the second year   37
7   Pasture management   43
8   Care of the youngster at grass   55
9   And into the third year   65
10 Showing   69
11 Growing pains   89
12 Feeding   101
13 Travelling   115
14 Routine servicing   127
15 Teeth   137
16 Learning   145
17 Minor ailments   157
18 Bitting   167
19 Conclusion   173

Index   175

FOREWORD

When Jane asked me to review this book and write a foreword to it I felt very honoured but also completely astonished. Why me? I am not a fellow equine 'guru', I am simply an enthusiastic amateur. However, after reading the manuscript I realised just why I had been asked. I am all the categories of people that the book is aimed at — rolled into one! Let me explain.

Years ago, I became the proud owner of a young Arabian gelding, my first horse. I was greener than the lush grass that Kashmir grazed in the Heronstream pastures. I did not have the help of this book then, but I did have the help of the author. All the advice and guidance that Jane gave me over the years (and some more) is contained here. I will always be indebted to her for this (and so will my horse!).

However experienced we may be with adult horses, young ones need different care if they are to enjoy their adolescence to the full and have the best possible start to their working life. Therefore, this is not a book aimed at the wise and experienced, this is for those of us who through sheer enthusiasm for our beloved horses and ponies, sometimes rush in where angels fear to tread — and often pay the penalty. It is also for the inexperienced amateur who wishes to do the best for their youngster but may not have the courage of their convictions.

Most of all, this is a book for the horses owned by all of us, as they are the ones which will benefit the most from Jane's wisdom and experience.

JULIE KIBBLE (*A somewhat wiser and more experienced — but still over-enthusiastic — one-horse owner!*)

Trimaroo aged one year. The faded ends to his mane and forelock, grown-out remains of the mane he was born with, are indications of his young age.

(*Opposite*) Olive enjoying a farm walk with two-year-old Shiny.

ix

PREFACE

First steps is a comprehensive guide for the increasing number of private owners who are bringing on their own young horse. For too long, the important, formative years of a youngster's life have been glossed over, and the owner is left wondering what is right or appropriate to do. Care of the in-foal mare and her new foal is well explained at all levels. There is plenty of literature on various methods of breaking and schooling the horse when it is old enough. This book endeavours to fill the gap left between these two parts in every horse's life, and takes the owner through all the important aspects relevant to the care and training of the young horse from the time it is weaned until it is ready to start work as a three year old. The care of the horse's physical as well as emotional needs are detailed, how it grows, learns and develops into a biddable young horse ready to cope with the additional demands of life as a riding horse.

Each aspect of the young horse's development is looked at, although a strict chronology is not always appropriate. Possible problems are also discussed. The emphasis is always on what is best for the horse, rather than most convenient. It is, above all, a practical book, for owners who are doing their horses themselves. Follow its guidelines well, and the young horse will have a foundation with lifetime benefits.

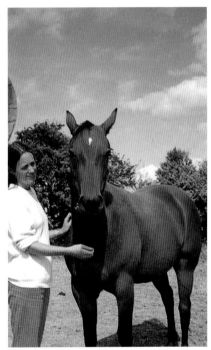

Elizabeth makes a careful check of her young horse.

(*Opposite*) A cautious approach of friendship between two yearlings — Justinus and Trimaroo.

ACKNOWLEDGEMENTS

This book could not have been written without the help, encouragement and tolerance of a great many people. I am especially indebted to my sister, Fliss, who threatened to write it herself if I did not; to Tony Hyett who spent many hours transcribing almost unintelligible scrawl into typescript; and to my parents whose faith in my ability really is beyond the call of parental duty!

Others who deserve thanks include the owners of horses I photographed, and also Val Cridge, Jackie Howe, Nancy Lawrence, Elizabeth O'Beirne-Ranelagh, Debbie Sewell, Lorna Freeman, Jackie Shanks, Jane Lake and Caroline Burt, Lucy Fletcher, Alec and Julia at *Essex Rider* and all those whose encouragement after *First foal* assured me I should write *First steps*.

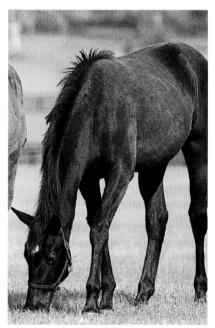

Weanling Thoroughbred at The Oaks.

(*Opposite*) Three-year-old Andrus.

1 INTRODUCTION: PROS AND CONS

Bringing on a youngster can be both rewarding and frustrating, fun and infuriating.

Although young horses are generally cheaper to buy than mature or 'made' ones, the cost of keeping them to an age when they are actually useful makes bringing on a young horse a very expensive exercise.

Of course, owning any horse is costly — the pleasure of horse-keeping is never cheap. A young horse will spend more time turned out and will not require your involvement in his exercise in the same way as a ridden horse, so you may well find that a youngster is much more economical on time. This is balanced, however, against the added risks involved with any young creature. Part of the learning process of developing maturity inevitably seems to involve risk-taking and ensuing accidents. So one's veterinary account could well be higher with a young horse.

At any stage of development, there is bound to be a percentage loss. The younger you acquire your horse, the greater the chance of loss: it may injure itself so badly as to be useless as a future riding horse; developmental problems may limit its usefulness, and its temperament may fail to match up to your ideal. In taking a backed and schooled horse, although the purchase price may be more, there is the benefit of having let someone else shoulder the risks as the horse grew up. But the reward of producing a sound, happy, healthy youngster ready to make its mark on the world is a great pleasure. If there is credit to be taken for its good looks, good behaviour and biddable temperament, you can take it all! Having survived

Yearling Triple Time.

(*Opposite*) Margaret visited the stud and viewed both parents and some of their relations before Chrysanda was born. When she was just one day old, the sale was confirmed. Three years later, Margaret is still delighted with her purchase! She did her 'homework' and was not disappointed.

the many pitfalls, you will have earned it.

So bringing on a youngster is fraught with problems, but the rewards can often be worth the effort.

2 ACQUIRING A YOUNG HORSE

There are two principal ways of acquiring a young horse. One is to breed your own, the other is to buy from a reputable stud. Alternatively, you can buy from sales or dealers, or privately from owners who have had to sell their youngster for some reason, such as financial problems or perhaps their inability to cope with the extra demands of a lively yearling or two year old, but these are not the routes of choice. In producing your own youngster, you will already have experienced the anxieties and pleasures of breeding, after which bringing on a youngster will be that much easier. Buying from a stud enables you to select the type, breed, colour, markings, sex and so on of your choice. Most studs are happy to take a deposit on a youngster almost from the day it is born – this really is the next best thing to breeding your own and far more sensible if one is to be purely practical about things.

To make the most of this situation and to be sure of having the widest choice, try to arrange to visit as many studs as possible during the winter months. Take in as much information as is available on likely sires and dams. It should also be possible to view older siblings of as-yet-unborn youngsters.

With observation and discreet enquiry it is possible to get a fairly accurate impression of the stock produced on certain studs or from particular lines. Some will be discarded and others listed as possible, so once the foals are born, time-wasting visits to studs which are unlikely to produce what you want are avoided. Having thus polarised your thoughts, it is just a matter of advising the stud owner of your likely interest and arranging to view the foals when they arrive.

A good one stands out in a crowd!

(*Opposite*) Children would have you buy everything! But do not take small children on your visits to studs unless, as here, you know the child is under control and the horses are good natured. Four-year-old Hannah instinctively gets down to Jongleur's level – the horse is not nervous, nor the little girl.

3

A nice-looking foal whose dam is clearly relaxed.

This mare is very back at the knee. This is considered a serious weakness likely to result in unsoundness.

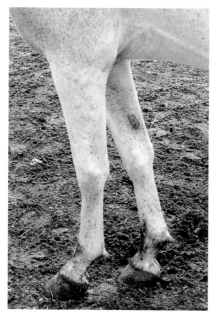

The sire and dam of your youngster should have provided it with the best start in life, which is genetic soundness. Both parents should have proved themselves to be sound – of temperament, conformation and performance. If they have already proved that they consistently pass these qualities on to their offspring, then so much the better. Proof of identity is not only nice to know but extremely important for future competition or breeding. It really is risky buying a youngster which is not registered. The pedigree can yield useful information which is not confined merely to the names of ancestors; research can reveal the performance records of those ancestors which will give you a valuable guide to your youngster's potential. Registration also provides proof of identity, ownership and breeding.

All new-born foals look gorgeous! But allow time to take stock: a good foal of any breed or type will be strong, steady and true on its limbs from the day it is born. Very many new-born foals are not straight limbed; in fact there are probably more foals that have some slight and temporary problem than those which are perfect from day one.

Although over-sloping pasterns, knock knees, marked cow hocks and standing very much on 'tip toe' may all go by the time the youngster is a week old, the one without these problems has got to be best; youngsters slow to correct problems are the ones to pass by.

Having made your choice, as with any other horse, do have it vetted. The younger the horse is, the less the vet is able to do, but at least (s)he can be sure your youngster is free from congenital defects and is sound in its heart, lungs and eyes. Later on, before starting ridden work, you may well feel inclined to have the horse 'vetted' again, for your own peace of mind before making strenuous physical demands of it.

Of course, you can buy young horses at any age, but you have the greatest choice when buying a foal and the greatest opportunity to influence its upbringing. Having made your choice, arranged the vetting (successful, we hope!) and then paid the deposit, all you do is wait until you can get it home. Most studs will be delighted for you to visit your youngster and get to know it before it is weaned. Try to avoid the temptation of talking for hours about your darling – stud owners are busy people!

The usual age for a foal to be weaned is six months. Later weaning can prove very beneficial, especially as the foal's large intestine will be unable to digest fibre effectively until it is around seven and a half months old. Do not be tempted, nor let the stud persuade you, to take delivery of your new foal too soon. Premature separation from its dam denies the foal the food, companionship and guidance only she can give. Vices such as cribbing, wind-sucking, weaving and box-walking can often be traced to weaning before the foal was physically or emotionally ready.

It is kinder to the foal to allow it to settle in familiar surroundings before it is taken to a new home, so preferably the stud from which you made your purchase will have weaned your foal a couple of weeks or at least a few days before you take delivery. However, a smaller establishment may find this difficult, if they have not the opportunity to move the mare out of sight and earshot of her distraught and shouting baby. In such a situation, it may be deemed more

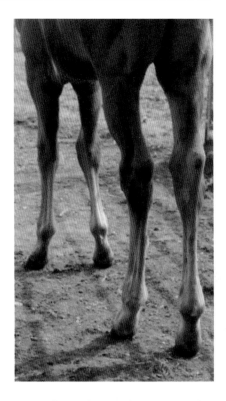

From this rather unflattering angle, the deviation in this foal's lower forelegs looks worse than it is. Slight toeing out normally corrects itself. The left foreleg appears straight through the knee; the right foreleg shows slight signs of deviation in the knee (carpal) joint which will need action taken if it does not correct in a month or so.

It will be three years yet before children will be able to start riding Bubbles of Rettendon, who is only nine months old, but while she is growing up Jackie will be kept busy bringing her on and taking her to a few shows.

convenient to send the foal away straight from the mare.

Some studs will travel the mare and foal together, leave the foal at its new home and take the mare home with them. This does have the advantage of ensuring that the foal has as stress-free a journey as possible, certainly if its dam is a seasoned and confident traveller. The mare and foal will be travelled together in a lorry in one, double sized, compartment. It will need full, solid partitions, with no gaps at the sides or along the bottom of the partition. In fact, the travelling stall is just like a small loose box. The mare is not tied up, because the foal could get caught in her lead rope. Neither of them will wear headcollars for the journey, again, because of the risk of getting caught.

It is much safer for the mare and foal both to be loose. However, in a trailer, there must be sufficient room for the mare to turn round, which she will do, as they always seem to prefer facing the back. If not, she will have to be tied up. In this case, tie her short, at eye height, to reduce the risk of the foal hanging itself should it go round the front of the mare.

When loading, always put the foal in first. This is easily achieved with two people, their hands linked behind the foal. The mare is able to see what is happening to her foal, will follow it into the transport, and is unlikely to panic.

The floor should be thickly bedded with their usual bedding material. On a long journey, a haynet can be provided, tied up very securely and at the maximum height to allow each to be able to eat from it. It is probably better to put this in at the first rest stop, when they have both had a chance to settle to the journey. If it is not a long trip, the dangers involved in providing a haynet are probably not worth it. Haynets, foals and journeys are not a happy mixture, the risk of an accident occurring being high. The haynet may drop as it empties, increasing the chance of the inquisitive foal getting a foot caught in it. Foals often chew, and it could also get the haynet caught in its mouth.

If your foal arrives by this method, offer the driver a drink, meal or whatever else is needed, and see to the paperwork (registration papers, vaccination certificate, any security details, money and receipts may need to change hands!) before unloading, because as soon as the foal is off the box, the driver will want to take the mare away with all haste to avoid further upset, as the newly separated pair will neigh frantically at each other, expressing their desire to be reunited. It may be necessary to unload both the mare and the foal, in order to get the foal into its new stable without too much fuss, and then the mare will be reloaded for her return. A sympathetic driver will stop to give her a rest and some water a few miles into the return journey.

If you are to collect your new acquisition from the stud or breeder yourself, choose a vehicle with a ramp which is not too steep. In fact, a trailer has the easiest ramp to negotiate for this, possibly the foal's first journey. It will be, in any case, anxious, never having left home on its own before. It will travel best in the same arrangements as for the mare and foal together, that is, a roomy compartment with full, safe partitions. In a trailer, take out all the fitments, such as partition, breast bar, and so on. The fixing points remaining should have their retaining pins inserted, and the whole fitment should

Once you have chosen your youngster, do not be in too much of a hurry to get it home. It will benefit far more by remaining with its dam until it is at least seven and a half months old. Jenerous, six and a half months old, November. Living out with feeds. Not yet weaned.

Mummy, can we have this one? If a young family is involved, good temperament is even more important when choosing your youngster. The unperturbed dam, quietly grazing in the background, gives a hint of this filly's future good nature.

be wrapped in adhesive tape for safety. Ensure that there is no possible way that the foal could open the groom's door from the inside. All the top doors will need to be closed, or, if there are no doors, the canvas shuttering lowered. The foal will, on this occasion, be best off travelling loose, as it is unlikely that it will have been taught to tie up and in any case will be too young to be restrained for the duration of a journey. Later, when you have educated it a little and it is bigger, it will be different. But now, it is safer to have it loose. It is absolutely vital that the driver is sympathetic and drives slowly and with great care. At such a young age, it is inappropriate to consider putting bandages on the legs. They will most likely slip, or at

Just-weaned Jaziyeh is learning to pose quietly for a photo. Debbie has a fascinating future ahead, bringing on her first, home-bred, youngster. Note the safe clothing, well-fitted headcollar and extra long rope.

least will be very uncomfortable to a youngster not accustomed to them. They could also be impossible to get on!

You may be tempted to travel in the box with the foal. Do not do this as it is dangerous and, in a trailer, illegal. In a lorry, it is usually possible to observe the precious cargo. In a trailer, a baby alarm can be fitted so you can hear if there is any trouble.

This will be an exciting and stressful day for you and the horse. Keep calm, and above all, be patient with your frightened foal, which is undergoing the biggest upheaval of its life.

3 A SAFE HOME

To make the most of its breeding and to enable it to fulfil at least some of its potential, a young horse needs a suitable environment in which to grow up and develop. It should be safe, to avoid risk of injury, but it should also be stimulating in order to encourage development physically and mentally.

Over winter, the vast majority of youngsters will need some form of housing. Even hardy native breeds will require shelter, if not man-made as such, at least natural in the form of shelter from trees, a thick hedge, woodland or even cliffs. The greater proportion of horses will be housed in traditional stables, but young horses especially do not always thrive emotionally on this enforced and unnatural form of solitary confinement. Large boxes can be successfully shared by two compatible youngsters — similar in age and sex, and neither especially dominant over the other. Importantly, similarity of size and type ensures that their dietary needs will also be very similar and, so long as one is not bullying the other, they can be cared for almost as one. Other less orthodox but nevertheless satisfactory ways of housing young horses include yarding them in a similar way to cattle, or providing access from the pasture to a large shelter or barn in which they are fed.

A young horse needs protection from severe weather. Generally, they do not have the bulk or fat of an older horse. Their weight to surface area ratio is less satisfactory for retaining warmth and in any case, demands are being made on the diet for growth as well as warmth. Youngsters are (and should be) lively and energetic and this, too, creates extra demands. To maintain condition in severe weather is too often not possible,

When fields become too wet, or the weather too awful, alternative means of exercise are necessary. These two Arab weanlings (Jongleur and Jenerous) are making good use of the covering yard out of season.

(*Opposite*) A large group of recently weaned foals in a purpose-built yard at the Welton Stud.

11

Chahara and Jongleur happily share a large stable for their first winter – watched from next door by Jenerous and Trickery. Stables separated by bars such as these are ideal for all horses, but especially youngsters.

hence the greater need of youngsters for shelter than mature horses. As with all stock, the real robber of condition is cold rain driven by a stiff wind. Not only is it directly chilling, but in such weather horses tend to stand huddled in the most sheltered place they can, standing with their heads low and tails to the wind. They will not be grazing so are suffering the double indignity of an increased requirement for food, combined with a disinclination to face the weather and go grazing.

Whatever housing is provided, it should be sufficiently spacious to allow the youngster to walk around freely and to roll without getting cast. Although not yet fully grown, he will still need the same size of stable as a youngster as he will require as a mature horse (see Table 1).

Table 1 Stable sizes

| Minimum size of stable | | Maximum size of horse |
Feet	Metres	
8 × 8	(2.3 × 2.3)	Shetland Pony
10 × 8	(3 × 2.3)	Exmoor, Welsh Mountain
10 × 10	(3 × 3)	New Forest, Connemara
10 × 12	(3 × 3.6)	Welsh Cob, Arab
12 × 12	(3.6 × 3.6)	Riding Horse, Small Hunter
12 × 14	(3.6 × 4.2)	Hunter, Warmblood

The floor itself should be reasonably non-slip and if it drains satisfactorily, so much the better. But if the drains are not satisfactory — if they don't work efficiently or are constantly getting obstructed — you may prefer to block them up and manage without. If you do have drains, make absolutely certain that small inquisitive hooves cannot possibly get trapped or caught, remembering that young horses seem blessed with a lot of imagination! The way in which walls and doors meet floors is important, too; no gaps into which hooves and even legs could extend when the youngster lies down or rolls over. The walls themselves must be strong enough to withstand kicking but not of an abrasive nature as young legs, especially hocks, are too easily scraped.

All studwork should be boarded over, with kicking boards to about 4 ft 6 in. (1.4 m) and something slightly less expensive such as ply board above that, where the problem is less one of kicking and more one of chewing. Smooth rendered or timber walls are also easier to keep clean. Pressure hosing is an

Communal living suits young horses. These two-year-old Welsh ponies are happily housed together in a large, airy pen at the Ada Cole Memorial Stables. These two had been abandoned on the motorway.

excellent way of cleaning stables but takes the mortar out of brickwork.

Rough plaster or breeze blocks are also difficult. Dirt gets trapped in the crevices making cleaning by any method hard work. Repainting is also very time consuming on unsuitable surfaces.

Traditional whitewash is no longer available, but exterior grade emulsion paint is just as good on the appropriate surfaces inside a stable. Timber is less likely to be chewed, as well as being protected from rotting, when treated with creosote. The lower two feet or so of solid walls can be painted with black bitumen which is damp repellent. Of course, following any painting or timber treatment, time must be allowed for it to dry. If the doors are secured in the open position, a through current of air will aid the drying process and also remove noxious fumes — a particular hazard with creosote. Thorough drying may take up to a week.

Doors should be wide enough to allow you and your horse to pass through in fairly close order, and the bottom half of the door (or gate on a yard) should be high enough to discourage unrequired bids for freedom and also discourage weaving.

Cage boxes with bars provide light, airy accommodation. They are especially good for young horses as they can see and touch their companions.

Sufficient height at the lintel reduces the risk of your youngster becoming headshy through hitting its head when admiring the view. A Thoroughbred, for example, may need 8 ft (2.4 m) to the door lintel, a door width of 4 ft 6 in. (1.4 m), and a bottom door height of at least 4 ft 6 in. (1.4 m).

The layout of the stabling requires some consideration if problems are to be avoided. The new weanling will feel very insecure, and will want and need company and contact with at least one companion. If that companion is only visible over the top door, then the young horse will be tempted to try to get over the door to reach the other horse. The best arrangement is to have a grille in the dividing wall between their two stables, so that they can see each other, and, if they want to, are able to touch each other, too. Some internal stabling systems can be excellent for young horses, as the bars which divide the stables above a height of about 4 ft 6 in. (1.4 m) allow the horses housed in them to be able to see and to touch their companions, as well as providing light and airy accommodation. It is very important, however, to ensure that the bars are not so wide as to allow a small hoof to become trapped between them. Such partitions can also be used with benefit as internal walls in traditional stabling systems.

On large yards with plenty of horses, it is possible to arrange matters so that a vulnerable youngster is never left on its own, but on small yards, or where perhaps only very few horses are kept, it is possible that the youngster may find itself alone, albeit only temporarily. In such a situation, it will attempt anything in its endeavours to rejoin its companions, and is very likely to try to jump out. In a cage type loose box, provided the bars are sufficiently close, it can come to no real harm, but in an outside box with a traditional half door, the temptation to jump out is beyond resistance. Such stables for a newly weaned foal, or in fact any horse lacking the necessary calmness to cope alone, should have either a top door or a full grid to close the space above the half door. A weaving grid or an additional bar across the doorway is not sufficient. When the horse is about to be left, the door should be closed before the other horse is taken out.

Recently weaned Bold Baron of Rettendon and Tammy (part Arab) are turned out with Polo to keep an eye on them!

It is absolutely vital that the youngster have suitable company, and it is worth considering just what is suitable! A young horse is a playful creature, and if the companion has some capacity for play, this will help the youngster to develop and to satisfy its need for practice fights, and pretend flights from imagined fears. It is not kind to ask a very old or unsound horse to have to cope with a young horse's boundless energy. The companion will be sharing the same pasture, so needs to be of a type that will not come to any harm on good grass. Ponies such as Shetlands, which are prone to laminitis, would thus be unsuitable company for a Thoroughbred. A baby horse has perhaps not yet learned all the niceties of equine etiquette, and its older chum will feel he needs to do some harsh explaining when it gets out of hand, so it is a wise precaution, for the first few weeks at least, to have the companion unshod, to avoid the risk of an unnecessary injury.

Newly weaned, the foal will still have a strong urge to suckle, and the younger it is, obviously, the stronger that urge will be. If weaning has been delayed until the foal is at least seven and a half months (this author's recommended minimum age for weaning), the foal will already have experienced the occasional rejection from its dam when it felt like a drink but she was not inclined to oblige. It will have learned to make its approaches a little more cautious, to check her mood. A younger foal is more indulged by its dam, who will be far more inclined to give up her grazing or her doze to allow her baby to suckle. Taken away from the dam, the weanling is very likely to see if its new companion will oblige as its dam had. Mare or gelding, the new friend will have its under-carriage checked out! Neither will be able to oblige, but it will probably get a sharper rebuff, in fact, from a mare. The younger the foal, the more likely it is that it will try to suckle its companion, the less likely it is to understand or react to its signals of displeasure at the overture, and so the greater the risk of the youngster's getting hurt. It is possible, in very rare circumstances, that a very maternally minded mare used as a companion in this situation could produce some milk for the 'weanling'. If she does, it will not be much, unless she herself has just been weaned from her own foal. It would, therefore

Trimaroo (one year) submits to Kadir (ten years) by lowering his head and neck; he is also baring his teeth and opening and closing his mouth as proof of his inferiority —

but Kadir is not interested and sends him on his way with a bite.

be a little unkind to ask her to babysit another foal.

So long as the weanling was not weaned too early, and so attempts to develop an unnatural relationship with its new friend, there should not be too much of a problem in choosing a suitable candidate. The most important consideration is that it has a good temperament and sets a good example of manners at feed time, catching up and turning out. Bad habits such as door kicking are very easily copied by an impressionable youngster.

Enjoying a social visit! Margaret regularly visited Chrysanda, aged about six months and as yet unweaned, before she brought her home.

Rising one-year-old colt with 26-year-old companion. This former garden has been safely fenced (note the electric wire above the rails). It is not only easy to keep an eye on these horses, but young Justinus has the opportunity to become used to traffic and pedestrians. This is a day-time only arrangement.

More serious are stable vices such as weaving, crib-biting and wind-sucking, all of which are quickly copied by a bright juvenile, with disastrous results. Weaving, a repetitive swaying back and forth, often involving the feet marching time or lifting and crossing on each swing of the head, puts strain on the fore legs. It also works off condition and can cause uneven wear on the fore feet. Crib-biting and wind-sucking both involve the horse swallowing gulps of air. In the former, the horse grasps hold of a solid object between the teeth, such as the door, fence or manger. With the latter, it merely arches the neck as it gulps. Such horses are prone to colic and digestive upsets. They are often poor doers. Once a horse has developed one of these vices, it is unlikely ever to be cured, and is seriously devalued. Every attempt should be made to keep young horses away from older horses with these vices.

Young horses are insatiably curious and will investigate everything within their reach. The stable should be free from anything which will suffer the unwanted attentions of inquisitive lips and teeth. Particularly dangerous are electrical fittings and wiring. Lights should be in solid bulkhead fittings, with a toughened glass casing protecting the lightbulb. The fitting itself should of course be well out of the horse's reach. All wiring should be safely contained within trunking (conduit), and, again, as far as possible, out of reach. Switches, which should be of a waterproof design, should be outside the stable in a position inaccessible to the horse, such as behind the top door, in the tack room or round the corner. It is sensible to have a power point, from which to run electrical equipment you never considered using before! This should be a solid, metal affair, protected with a screw-on cover.

The water supply always comes in for a lot of attention from immature horses (and some grown-up ones, too). Buckets, inevitably, will double as footballs. It is dangerous to have buckets with handles on them in the stable, so if this is the only way to provide water, remove the handles from the water buckets, and use others with handles on them to take the water to the stable. Standing buckets inside an old motor tyre can render them somewhat less easily moveable. Automatic drinking systems can be very satisfactory, as the bowls are strong and securely bolted to the wall, but the pipes supplying the water will be chewed and pulled by the inmate.

Seven-and-a-half-month-old Cruise was weaned last week and has settled down well, so he has been turned out with the ten-year-old gelding Kadir — but he's not going to let his new friend go too far away! Newly weaned youngsters will naturally feel vulnerable and this should be accepted.

Even if it does not actually make a hole in the pipe, the youngster is very likely to pull the pipe out of its fittings. If the supply line is well above the height it can reach, the down pipe to the individual drinker can be dropped through a length of scaffolding pipe, where it will be safe.

All projections in the stable are a potential hazard and should be dealt with. Anything moveable will be moved, kicked and stamped on. Plastic bowls or buckets will have holes stamped in them, and can even end up on the horse's leg, with a nasty injury resulting.

Door catches can prove very attractive to prying lips. Use safety bolts at the top of the door, which are usually (but not always) horse proof, and a kick-over bolt at the bottom. Remember always to use both! If you feel the need to use a clip to prevent the top bolt from being undone, make sure it is of a safe design (see illustration on p. 33). Do not padlock the door as it will hinder a rapid release in the event of a fire. For security, padlock the yard gate, and ensure that the stable area is enclosed at all times.

Three-year-old colt in a well-sheltered, safely fenced paddock. He is wearing a headcollar — a wise precaution with entires — with a loop of string, which is an alternative to the safety loop on the tie ring.

4 LESSONS FOR THE FIRST YEAR: NOW CATCH YOUR HORSE

Acquiring a young horse is the beginning of the rewarding process of 'bringing on a youngster'. Many would like to do it and some have the opportunity to turn their dreams into reality.

But just what is involved in turning a newly acquired, recently weaned and probably just a bit frightened foal into a sound, confident and capable riding horse of the future?

It is possible that the youngster is not even all that familiar with being caught. Before the vitally important lesson of being tied up is learnt, you must be able to put on the headcollar quickly and without trouble. You should also be able to lead and release the youngster without problems.

As a foal at the stud, the youngster would have been approached from the side or even the rear, having first been tactfully manoeuvred into a position of at least restricted escape. This may have been, for instance, a wedge shape formed by holding the dam at an angle to the gate or a safe fence. So, repeat the scenario. Avoid approaching your youngster in the middle of the field (or even the stable) but try to approach where at least some lines of escape are blocked by the fence, gate, wall or even a steady companion held by an assistant. Always approach slowly and never head on. If a youngster tenses ready to flee, be still for a moment until he relaxes or is ready for you to approach more closely. Aim for his shoulder and, when you get there, quietly run your hand and arm over his withers. From the near side this will be your right arm.

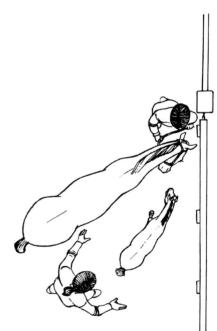

Bird's-eye view of the mare and handler forming a 'V' with the gate or safe fence. The foal can be quietly encouraged into the diminishing space where all escape routes are barred, and thus caught. All parties must remain calm and confident throughout the procedure.

21

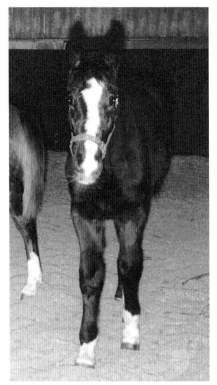

DJ (Hanoverian) wears a headcollar until he is convinced of the merits of being easily caught!

Hold the headcollar in your left hand out of the way. Pat him and rub him gently. Quietly draw the rope around his neck to hold him should he jump forward and also to keep it away from his legs. Then pass the headpiece of the headcollar under his neck from your left hand to your right hand, so that the headcollar is almost in position below his head. Keep your body as far back as possible. Slip the noseband quickly and quietly over his nose from underneath and then buckle it up. Until catching up has been easily established, it can be very helpful to leave the headcollar on the foal. It is important to make sure it fits comfortably and will not rub. The noseband must be sufficiently loose so as not to rub the jaws during feeding or grazing, sufficiently high so it cannot be pushed down and over the muzzle, but not so high as to rub the projecting cheek bones. A leather headcollar is ideal as it is less likely to rub than a nylon one and will break in an emergency, for instance if the horse becomes caught on something. However, leather is expensive and will need cleaning and oiling with neatsfoot oil from time to time (at least once a month) to keep the leather soft and waterproof. It is possible to compromise with a nylon headcollar fitted with a leather head strap (the top strap, which passes over the poll and buckles below the left ear). If a nylon headcollar is used, it should have a proper brass buckle with a steel pin, which will break under excessive strain. Nylon headcollars with rocko buckles (the sort that thread through and over) should never be used as there is no weak point to break in an emergency. Eight inches (20 cm) or so of plaited baler twine fitted to the lowest ring of the headcollar will form a convenient 'handle' to help catch the most difficult cases, but the temptation to grab at a fleeing foal should be resisted as it may only worsen an already difficult situation.

Once safely in the stable, take the headcollar off and replace it again, to accustom the foal to your handling him around the head. While doing this, keep the lead rope round his neck, so you can keep some hold on him should he shy away. Gradually you will find that the headcollar can be left off in the stable, and eventually in the field too, unless yours is one of the few who will always be awkward to catch!

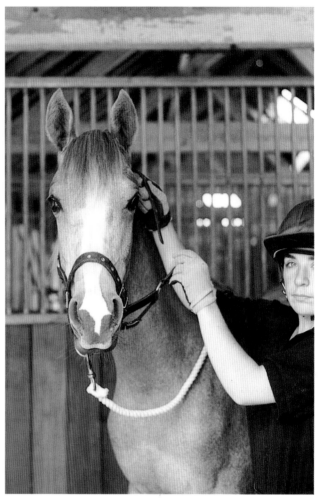

Should the youngster be reluctant to lead, always push from behind, never pull from in front. It helps to have an assistant walking a safe distance behind, quietly encouraging him forward, whilst of course remaining within the horse's field of vision and keeping out of range of any kicks.

Many and various methods have been suggested to help encourage difficult cases to lead well, mainly involving rope or lunge lines in a variety of configurations behind or around the animal. None of these is to be recommended. Firstly, not all people are in a position to have the necessary extra people to help them. Secondly, there is always a great risk that the horse will not respond 'correctly'. Many green youngsters

(*Left*) When catching a horse, put the rope over the neck first.
(*Right*) Notice that Jackie keeps to the side of yearling Trickery, and holds both the buckle and the head strap of the headcollar. This prevents buckles or ends flicking, which could frighten or even injure the horse.

will instinctively lash out with the hind legs if they feel something unexpected around their legs or hindquarters. Ropes which slip can cause nasty accidents and put both the horse and its handler at risk. The greatest help in encouraging compliance is to avoid at all costs pulling from in front or looking the horse in the eye. Humans have the eyes of predators, close together on the front of the face, giving them clear, binocular vision. Instincts will be ringing warning bells for the horse faced with such a threatening (to it) look. The horse's eyes are those of a typical victim – wide apart, at the sides of the head, offering a wide field of vision, but with little binocular sight. Thus horses can pick up danger sooner, and have a greater chance of successfully avoiding a conflict.

The horse's limited binocular vision, in which objects are seen with both eyes, is in the sector immediately ahead. The wide range seen with only one of the eyes is not so clear and distances are less easy to judge. Should something attract the horse's attention in a zone seen with only one eye, it may well wheel around, backing up if necessary, in order to view it with both eyes. Seeing with both eyes, it will be able to see more clearly and also judge the size and distance more reliably. This is why our approach to a nervous or young horse should not be rushed. The youngster must have time to assess us and, we hope, reach the conclusion that we pose no danger. If it is felt by the horse that something seen with one eye could be a threat, it will flee, escaping from the possible danger.

The wide range of vision is not complete. There are blind spots. An important blind spot is behind the horse's hind legs. Anything felt or suspected in this area will instinctively be kicked, hence the need always for caution around a horse's hind legs.

There is a further blind spot on the front of the horse's face, between the eyes. This blind spot is larger on horses with very wide or prominent foreheads. Those familiar with horses know from experience that it is very unusual for a horse to respond favourably to being patted on the forehead. They prefer to be patted on the neck, where one eye can see what is going on. An attempt to pat a horse on the front of its face usually results in it shying back, in an attempt to put the

Although Caramel has not seen me before, she does not feel threatened because I am standing where she can see me clearly.

It is always rewarding when the youngster is waiting expectantly for your visit! Blue is lucky to have a suitable gate of excellent design, based on right angles and avoiding any acute angles between the braces and bars where a young horse could trap a hoof.

person, or at least their hand, back into its field of vision.

There is yet another blind spot at the end of the muzzle and extending under the jaws. So important is it for a horse to know what is happening in this vital area, that the muzzle is endowed with long, tactile ('feeler') hairs so that objects in this area can be felt where they cannot be seen. There are similar hairs above and below the eyes. As these hairs all 'see' where the eyes cannot, it is important to the horse that they are left intact to do their vital work. The removal of tactile hair for showing, for instance, has to be regarded as an unnecessary unkindness, if not an actual cruelty.

By approaching the horse with due regard for how it sees us, and enabling it to keep us in view, it is possible to build a young horse's confidence when being caught in the field or stable. If the approach is always made towards the shoulder, the handler is less likely to be kicked, and the horse less likely

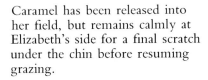

Caramel has been released into her field, but remains calmly at Elizabeth's side for a final scratch under the chin before resuming grazing.

to be confused or frightened by the person passing into and out of the field of vision. Encourage the horse to walk on by remaining as close to the nearside shoulder as possible, and looking yourself in the direction you wish to take. Use your voice firmly and with encouragement as you tell the horse to 'Walk on!'. An extra long rope will provide enough spare to flick the horse as far back as your left hand will reach. A companion horse or pony taken past the reluctant youngster will nearly always give it a successful lead. Horses are herd animals and will follow older members of that herd. A youngster will naturally copy the example set by another, more confident horse. This is the most satisfactory method of training. After a few days of following a lead, the young horse can be encouraged to go first, but with the company in close attendance and prepared to take the lead if necessary.

Letting the youngster go is also very important. We need to teach it to be patient and not to run off immediately. It will be easier to catch next time if its last contact with you was quiet and rewarding. Always let go facing the door or gate. Keep it steady and, ideally, distracted by scratching the favourite itchy spot. Let it go by reversing the procedure for putting the headcollar on. As you take the noseband off, tell it to '*Wait*' in a firm way and restrain it with your arms and the rope round the neck. If it remains for a moment or two to 'talk' to you after you have let go, you can congratulate yourself on a job well done. Never encourage any horse to gallop away from you.

When you go into and out of the stable, it must learn to give you sufficient space to do so. Teach it always to get back from the door. Push on the underneck or chest to get it to back and if it doesn't, pinch the skin and repeat your command 'back' a bit louder. Reward a correct response with praise. Also use 'back' (and expect a result!) when you put in the hay or feed.

Personally, I do not approve of feeding tit-bits from the hand. It makes all youngsters and especially colts very nippy and pushy. However, it can help catch a shy youngster. The aim is always that they should learn to come when called. The expectation of an immediate reward may help this. It will also be helpful if the horse had a reward when you turned it out. Pausing for a while to eat a carrot or handful of cubes as the headcollar comes off is a good way to encourage a positive response at catching-up time. Rewards should be presented in a bucket or bowl, rather than feeding from the hand.

No youngster likes to be left alone, so the sight of all its chums being caught, rewarded and removed should also help persuade it that it, too, wants to be caught, but *never* remove them all, leaving the youngster alone. Keep the last one held by the gate and, if necessary, use it to help catch the youngster in the same way as the dam before he was weaned.

Once these basics of catching, leading and turning out are mastered, the youngster is ready to be taught to tie up and be led in a more refined way, suitable for showing, or presenting to a vet, for example.

Two-year-old Arab fillies keeping close to each other on their first day out at their new home.

Correctly and safely tied up.
Headcollar: correctly fitted, ends all tucked in, noseband has plenty of room for comfort in the stable, but is high enough so it cannot slip over the nose.
Rope: a quick release knot, short enough to avoid the risk of injury, and the rope long enough so that the horse cannot reach the end.
Tie ring: at eye level, this is as high as margins of safety dictate. A single loop of string will break in the event of the horse panicking. The tie ring is secured to a strong, solid upright.

5 FURTHER FIRST YEAR LESSONS: TYING AND GROOMING

Once the youngster has learned the basics of stable manners and is confident at being caught, led and let go, it is time to teach it to be groomed and to tie up. This can be done when it is still with the dam, but here we are assuming your youngster is weaned and probably recently acquired!

Learning to stand whilst being groomed and tying up are lessons which can be taught concurrently. It is very important that the youngster (or any horse for that matter) is restrained when you have things to do with it. It is grooming now but later it could be the vet, farrier and eventually a rider who will want it to stand quietly while the necessary tasks are done. If you start grooming without some form of restraint (tying up or having someone else to hold it) it will very quickly realise that if it does not suit, it can wander off and there is nothing you or anyone else can do about it. A horse that won't tie up is often 'bargy' as well, for it knows it can get its own way. So at first for grooming, with one hand you may hold the youngster by the headcollar rope, quite close so it can't wander round, and with the other hand groom the bits you can reach. In reality, this will not amount to much more than the neck and shoulders. Don't be afraid to use a stiff brush — a dandy brush is often accepted more readily than a body brush. Youngsters are often a bit itchy and the bristly dandy brush feels good; a soft brush can just annoy. Quite why youngsters should enjoy a good scratch more than older horses remains a puzzle. Certainly, when they are changing their coat they can be itchy. Perhaps their thin, young skin is more sensitive as the nerve endings will be nearer the surface. So long as the

Early lessons in standing soon pay off. Three-year-old Andrus poses beautifully for a picture at home on the lawn.

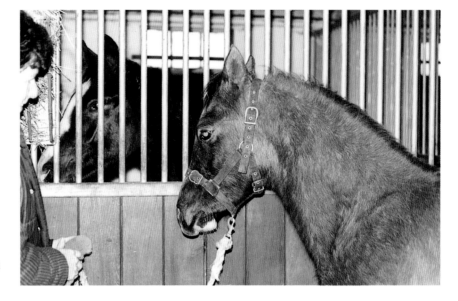

Recently weaned foals DJ (Hanoverian) and Je'phari (Arab) can see and 'talk' to each other through the bars in these internal stables. This is an excellent system for young horses.

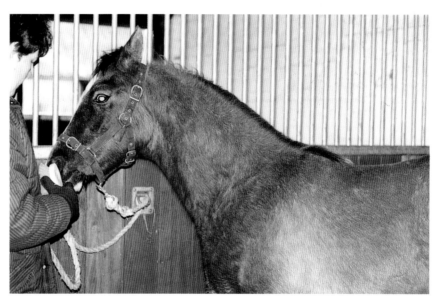

For the first tying lesson, the rope is passed through the tying ring, but held, not knotted.

problem is not due to parasites such as lice, or some other skin disorder such as ringworm, this itchiness can be accepted as normal.

To reach the sides and hindquarters, you will need a longer rope, passed through the tie ring and back to your hand. Soon the pupil will realise it is 'tied up'. Should it try to pull back, a pat on the hindquarters with gentle verbal encouragement

For the first grooming sessions, hold the weanling's lead rope in one hand, and groom as far as you can reach with the other. Note companion the other side of the bars — they can see and touch each other.

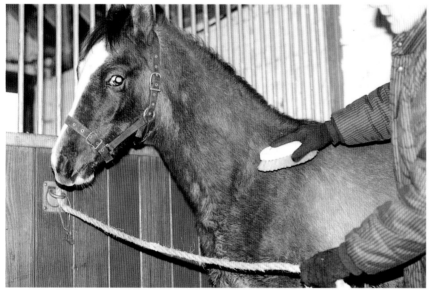

Je'phari (eight months) was weaned last week. Here, he learns to stand for grooming while Lorna is well away from his head, but holding the long rope through the ring.

('*No!*' or '*Come on, up!*') will soon stop it. Remember, it is not yet very strong. Before long it will be much stronger and more determined, so make the most of the relatively small size and lack of muscle power. Once this stage has been accepted, tie it up properly with a quick release knot. The use of a loop of safety string is a debatable point. If the horse is not a panicky type, it can be better to tie directly to a strong ring before he realises that a sharp tug is rewarded with freedom! But nervy, panicky types which take fright and pull back wildly in fear are better with the rope tied to a small loop of string attached to the ring, the string breaking should the horse panic. You must use your judgement. The tie ring must be strong and firmly fixed. If it could be pulled off the wall, or come away complete with the board to which it is screwed, then use the string loop. Better that the string breaks than the horse pulls down the wall or the fence.

Tying up should be confined to the stable until the horse has become totally reliable. A young horse should never be tied up outside on the yard, to the fence in the field, or anywhere else it could be startled by a bird, traffic, or even people walking by. Should this happen, and the horse panics and pulls back, it could slip and injure itself, or even break whatever it was tied to and run away, attached to the damaged remains of the fence or whatever. In the stable, there is the protection of the bedding, less chance of the horse being startled, and provision of a suitable and well-maintained tying point. No horse should ever be tied up on a bare concrete surface.

The tying ring should be at a suitable height, which is between the level of the horse's chin and its eye when standing normally. If it is too high, the headcollar will be pulled round, and the discomfort may cause the youngster to pull away. It could also injure the eye. Too low, and the downward pressure will cause the horse to throw up its head, and again, pull back. There is also an increased chance that it could get a fore leg over the rope. If the horse can stand comfortably when it is tied up, compliance is much more likely, and the risk of an injury resulting from the horse's objecting is greatly reduced.

The tying ring should be well away from the door, so the horse cannot look over the door when it is tied up. This avoids the possibility of its knocking its head on the door jamb or lintel. Also, it helps ensure that the horse is concentrating on what is being done to it, and is aware of what is going on, and not distracted by other matters outside the stable. The tying ring should be very firmly anchored by bolting it right through the wall to a plate on the other side,

A safe tying ring, recessed into the wall, fixed to 1 inch (2.5 cm) hardwood boarding, and with a loop of string to tie to. The blue tape acts as a 'silencer' as the ring in its housing had a tendency to rattle noisily.

or at least ensuring that it is screwed securely in to the stud-work, not just on to the planking or cladding. Check that there is maximum headroom over the ring, and that it is not positioned beneath a roof strut or a beam, which the youngster could hit with its head should it panic and rear up.

Confine tying up to the time when the horse is being groomed, for instance. Do not tie it up for too long, and do not go away, leaving it on its own, when it is tied up.

Most economically priced lead ropes on sale in saddlery shops are supplied with a plated steel spring clip. If such a clip must be used, do ensure that the spring part of the clip faces away from the jaw. Should the horse pull back, spring clips done up the wrong way round can very easily hook into the soft skin of the underjaw or chin, causing a nasty tear wound which can even include the lips. It is more satisfactory to use the slightly more expensive, but infinitely safer, brass trigger clips which cannot get caught in the horse's flesh. Clips used for securing the top bolt of the door against inquisitive lips undoing it should also be of the trigger type, never the spring clip, as in this situation they can get caught in the tongue, ripping it horrifically as the horse pulls back from the pain.

The rope itself also needs to be appropriate. Do not tie up using cotton or nylon webbing, as it will not release quickly in an emergency, and can be difficult to undo in any situation if the knot has tightened. Cotton ropes are probably the best as they are comfortable to the hand, pliable, and will break in an emergency. They are not very long lasting and are prone to fraying, however. Lead ropes made of artificial fibres may tend to unravel or fray. Such ropes are frequently sealed at the end, by the manufacturer, with a plastic keeper. These are very dangerous. The slight extra weight of the plastic acts as a pendulum, and a loose or swinging rope end can flick up, causing a nasty injury to the horse or the handler. Eyes are especially vulnerable.

Lead ropes should be in good condition, free from knots, frays or loose and unravelled portions. Slippery ropes do not hold knots well and are more likely to cause rope burns. Natural fibres such as cotton or sisal are best. Ends should be whipped, bound or neatly back spliced, but never knotted. A

From the left:
(1) Potentially dangerous spring clip on a good cotton rope;
(2) Good trigger clip with a nylon web lead rein, which can cause nasty burns and is almost impossible to tie up safely;
(3) Good sisal rope hand spliced on to a good trigger clip;
(4) Cotton rope safely (but inconveniently) slotted on to headcollar.
(5) Softish nylon rope hand spliced on to a good trigger clip;
(6) Stiff and unyielding polypropylene rope hand spliced on to an unsafe spring clip.

Types of lead ropes and clips (from left):
(1) Cotton rope with brass trigger clip. Cotton handles well and is soft, but wears out quickly. This is the safest clip.
(2) Sisal rope with eyelet instead of clip. Safer than a clip, but not convenient if you want to take the rope off quickly. Sisal is harder wearing than cotton, and this one is thick enough to give a good grip. Hand spliced.
(3) Brass spring clip 'recycled' on to synthetic rope after its original lead rein (note square eyelet) wore out. This rope is hard and stiff, and cheap.
(4) The worst sort of clip. Spring clips can get caught on the horse, and the large ring can injure the unthinking handler who slips a finger into it. Same rope as (3), hand spliced on to a re-used clip.

knotted end can be dangerous in the same way as the plastic keeper, and can also become caught up, causing a horse to panic. Should a horse you are leading with a knotted rope pull away from you, the knot catching into your hand can result in a nasty injury or even a broken finger.

Until your youngster has learned to tie properly, it is not advisable to start grooming the legs, belly or tail, unless you have an assistant to hold it. Most youngsters will kick out when you first groom the belly, tail or hind legs. It is a natural reaction, but with tact and care it can be avoided. Handling the fore legs (especially with colts) can result in the youngster dropping down on to his knees or even falling over. It is a form of submission, but rather disconcerting! Colts playing (or fighting) often bite at each other's lower fore legs in an attempt at disablement. When you initiate this reaction, be tactful, because you do not want inadvertently to trigger 'horse-play'. You must always be your young horse's superior, never its play-mate or sparring partner.

A touchy horse may settle if it gets used to the contact of your hand before you use a brush. Use firm pressure and don't remove your hand at the first twitch or reaction. Persist, and the horse should soon settle. It can't come to much harm (it is tied up) and you can make progress however slowly without causing alarm. It is a good idea to wear a hard hat, especially with colts — you'll be amazed how far the feet can reach — and even stifles and knees can cause a great deal of pain should they come down on your head!

Limbs should be groomed only with a leather-backed body brush. Inadvertent knocks with wooden brushes can bring up bony lumps resembling splints which can be sore and painful for the horse and a great disadvantage in the show ring. It is also important not to discourage the youngster at this stage by carelessly or accidentally causing it pain.

Handling the feet often causes problems, but need not. Running your hand down the fore leg often makes the horse pick up the foot anyway, so as you start sliding your hand down from the shoulder, with fairly light pressure this time, command 'Up' and as you go past the knee the chances are it will pick up the foot. Grasp the hoof — not the fetlock, pastern or cannon, just the actual hoof. Holding on to the leg may result in the horse kneeling down or even falling over, for the reasons mentioned above. Also, by holding the hoof, you have a mechanical advantage over the horse, due to your being at the furthest point of his leg, which is in effect a lever.

Hold the foot quite low to the ground, so it is between fetlock and knee height, just long enough to keep it still for a short moment. Then quietly replace the hoof to the floor, and gently praise and reward the horse. Repeat with the other fore hoof. The next day you'll be able to pick the hooves out more quickly and by the end of the week you'll both be old hands! Hind feet sometimes react similarly to the fore feet, and sometimes they lash out. If it kicks keep clear so you don't get hurt. Let the horse kick the wall instead! Avoid wrapping your arm round the leg (to avoid risk of serious injury such as a broken arm or dislocated shoulder) or holding on above the hoof which will irritate the horse more and is mechanically disadvantageous.

Be persistent and be firm but don't get into a fight. Should your youngster lean into you or even try to sit on you (that is just what it feels like!) be extra firm – if it were nervous, it would be trying to get away from you, not pushing into you. If it won't let you lift the hoof, be content for it to ease the weight on that foot as a start to allowing you eventually to lift it in a few days' time. If it rests it, you can start to pick it out, even if it is just the heels of the hoof. Make progress each day and make sure you keep yourself out of trouble. A common mistake is to try to hold the hoof with your arm behind the leg – if he kicks, he takes your arm with him. Keep your arm the cannon bone side of the hind leg, as opposed to the tendon side (i.e. the anterior side of the leg; see photo).

At first keep grooming sessions fairly short and to the point. It will be most satisfactory if there is not the distraction of having hay or other feed. You want the horse to concentrate on what you are doing and to learn its lessons, such as moving over when you put a hand on its side and say 'Over' (the very first turn on the forehand!). It will learn to pick up its feet as you touch the top of his leg and say 'Up'. In all, it will learn to be willing and polite. But it will be hard for any

By keeping her right arm the anterior side of Koppelia's leg, Lorna avoids the risk of injury should the horse kick out. Hoof pickings are collected in the skip.

youngster to concentrate for more than ten minutes, or if it is hungry, due a feed, about to be turned out or if there are other horses being fed or turned out at that moment. If this is the case, delay the lesson until a more opportune time, finishing what you are doing as soon as possible and on a good note.

It will learn to stand more patiently if it is facing away from the door. If horses see space, they have an urge to try to get to it, so avoid temptation and keep it facing the wall.

These early lessons not only teach the youngster to tie up and be groomed, but they also set the standard for manners and compliance for the rest of its life. It will accept the things that you ask because you are the boss, you are firm and you are fair. Above all you are pleased and praise good behaviour.

The first winter: provided they are well fed, horses can thrive in even quite harsh conditions. Eight-month-old Comet is doing fine in the snow with his dam, Sky.

INTO THE SECOND YEAR

By the time the young horse's first birthday comes (most foals are born in April and May) it will hopefully have learned all the basic requirements of routine management. Catching, leading, tying up, grooming, standing for the farrier and turning out should by now come easily. Do not expect it always to be quiet about these things! Like any young creature, a young horse will be spooky, playful and sometimes naughty. This is normal and to be welcomed. If it is quiet now, then by the time it is adult, it will be so dull as to be a very boring riding horse — and probably hard work for the rider, too! Even so, whatever the excuse or provocation, do not allow the youngster to be dominant or aggressive towards you. Any attempt at over-stepping these limits should be dealt with firmly and fairly. Carry a whip when leading and be prepared to use it swiftly and firmly at the moment of misdemeanour. If a horse needs correcting it should never be done when you are in a bad temper or feeling frightened or nervous. A thrashing is rarely justified; one short correction with a sharp verbal warning should suffice. Never entice a horse into a fight — it is bigger, stronger and more deadly than you. Be fair and you will be respected: the horse will be safe to handle. Be unreasonable and you will be feared. A high-couraged horse, especially a stallion, may one day try to get his revenge. Such a horse is always dangerous.

Once these basic lessons are established, the best care the yearling can now have is to be turned away, that is turned out to grass for the summer. This is not to say he is to be neglected, for there is still a lot of growing to be done. If

Yearling Jenerous has recently been gelded, and is still sometimes nippy. Janice holds her whip in her right hand, across his muzzle, to prevent this.

An older horse sets the youngsters a good example. Here, Flyer gives a lead to Justinus, Jamborino and Trimaroo — all yearlings.

suitable conditions can be found, a summer at grass can be good for the horse nutritionally, emotionally (horses are happiest out of doors) and socially — dominant older horses will assure him of his lowly place in the order of things and set an example of good behaviour.

The youngster will be unshod and it is best if his companions at grass are similarly shoe-free, at least on the hind feet. An inquisitive youngster does not always react quickly enough to the threatening gestures of a dominant horse and will get bitten and kicked many times before learning to keep out of trouble.

This time spent turned out at grass is of vital importance to young horses. They can grow at a natural rate, and the almost constant exercise will go a very long way to helping develop strong bones and healthy muscles. Bone only hardens in response to pressure; standing in a stable will not produce strong bones, however good the diet. Similarly, muscles will only develop tone and fitness in response to use. Idle horses can gain weight with fat, but will never develop good musculature.

Turning a youngster away may give the impression that one is doing nothing, but, out on a good acreage, with room to gallop and the company of other horses for socialising as

Justinus (one year) approaches Flyer (four years) cautiously and with his head lowered submissively.

well as education, the horse cannot have a better start in life. The horse may not need a lot of time spent on it, but it is vital that the pasture is well cared for if it is to provide the best benefit.

Companionship is vital for the normal development of a young horse, and this presents no problem when several horses are kept together. Taking one horse out for a ride, for instance, will not leave the baby without a sitter! But where only a few horses are kept, or even where the youngster is one of only two, problems can arise if the other horse has to go for any

A raised leg and a swish of Flyer's tail has sent Justinus retreating submissively — but he'll be back again soon!

The third from the right is a four year old, the rest yearlings.

reason. If this absence is to be permanent, then obviously a replacement must be found. If it is only temporary, it need not cause too much upset if a little care is employed. In traditional stables, shut the top door on the youngster before the other has to leave, so it does not see it go and try to follow it. If it is fed at this time, this will give it a further distraction.

The youngster can be prepared for odd moments of loneliness by, for instance, being brought in from the field first. Some food in the stable will help again. Gradually, lengthen the gap between its coming in and the other coming in, but only when a short gap has been accepted first. It will also become gradually used to the notion of occasionally being away from other horses if it is brought out on its own from time to time for some leading practice, or grazing in hand, for instance.

Do not consider bringing up a young horse on its own. It is unkind and is very likely to result in serious behavioural problems, such as stable vices, or over-excitement when it does see other horses, followed by panic or even hysteria when it has to part from them. It is better not to have a youngster in these circumstances, or it should be liveried at a suitable yard with appropriate facilities for young horses, such as plenty of good, safe, well-fenced grazing. Alternatively, you could offer a 'foster' home to a horse or pony rescued by a welfare organisation, thereby helping not only your own but a horse in need, too.

Whilst many horses have to adapt as best they can to a solitary life, it is infinitely more beneficial to provide company, at least during the important formative years. There can never be any substitute for the comfort of the companionship of its own kind to a young horse.

Mutual grooming between yearling Blue and twelve-year-old Banjo. This enjoyable and beneficial activity is of course impossible for a solitary horse.

7 PASTURE MANAGEMENT

It is generally accepted that grazing horses require an acre of land each, plus a spare acre. Thus, for instance, five horses would need six acres. This acreage is best divided into two or even three paddocks so that some of the land can be rested at any one time. The smaller subdivision will be grazed more evenly, because the grass will be eaten down more quickly, less will get coarse and the familiar patch-work effect of ungrazed, dunged-on 'roughs' and closely grazed 'lawns' is less likely to develop. As the land is providing the horse with exercise space, as well as meeting nutritional requirements, the paddocks should be large enough to allow the youngster to stretch out into an extended canter or gallop.

Worm dosing of all horses should be timed to coincide with paddock changes. Thus a rested, relatively worm-free paddock will have relatively worm-free horses put on to it. This system of dividing pasture and alternately resting and grazing the paddocks is good pasture management: it also ensures that your young horse has access to fresh, quality grass without an undue risk of worms to which all horses, and especially those under four years old, are so prone.

It is almost inevitable that, as the summer goes on, weeds will start to become more and more obvious. They are a problem on any pasture, but always seem worse in fields used by horses because horses are such fussy grazers. For many people, spraying with weedkiller is not an acceptable option. It is also wasteful, because 'weeds' which could be beneficially consumed are killed, along with those recognised to be either harmful or unwanted. Many weeds which are

Jaz turned out in the autumn on clean pasture which has been rested for many months.

(*Opposite*) Jamborino, Trimaroo and Justinus. Three contented yearlings in a suitable field: shelter, safe fencing and no tall weeds.

ignored when growing become very acceptable when wilted and are often valuable sources of nutrients, but not when drenched in herbicide.

Just to the left of centre is a ragwort plant. This poisonous weed of pastures can be very hard to spot at this stage; seconds later it had been pulled out to be burnt.

A tall plant of hemlock growing next to a brook. Deadly poisonous! Note the distinctive smooth stem with purplish blotches.

The deadly hemlock (right) as distinguished from its innocuous cousin cow parsley (left).
Typically, it is growing on a brook bank.

Woody nightshade, also known as bittersweet: poisonous but not deadly.

Woody nightshade, growing with bramble against a hawthorn hedge next to a ditch — a typical habitat.

Black nightshade. Not a deadly poison, and unlikely to be eaten by other than starving horses.

Topping is ecologically sound and can provide nutritional benefits to the horses. It involves mowing or cutting the weeds and coarse grass and can be done with a tractor-mounted topping mower (more robust but less refined than a hay mower), an ATV (all terrain vehicle) fitted with a mower attachment, a strimmer or even by hand using a scythe.

Tractor-mounted topping mower. Topping is an ideal way to help control these buttercups and encourage grass growth.

However, before starting to do any topping, the area should be closely inspected for poisonous plants. Many toxic plants are ignored by grazing livestock so long as they are alive and growing. Once cut and wilted, perhaps due to losing their smell, they will be eaten, with obvious undesirable effects. Different poisonous plants grow in different situations. For instance, in the main areas of the field, in the open, ragwort is the main hazard. Near ditches and streams, one might find hemlock. Deadly, woody, white and black nightshades are more likely to be located under hedges.

One exception to this general rule of wilted poisonous plants being of a greater risk than live ones is the acrid buttercup. Its poison makes it bitter, hence the name, but once it wilts, the toxin changes to become tasteless and harm-less. Should it be eaten whilst growing, it is poisonous but not deadly. It it only likely to be grazed if the alternative for the stock is starvation, as it tastes awful. Other poisonous plants are also harmful when the grazing has been exhausted. Starvation may force the stock into taking, say, ragwort but also, in wandering around looking for grass, there is a greater risk of poisonous plants getting trampled. Once trampled, they wilt; once wilted, they will be eaten. Hemlock is a swift dispatcher; ragwort poisoning gradually destroys the liver. Its effects are cumulative over the animal's life. Death will eventually occur after prolonged suffering marked by stagger-ing, colic and weight loss.

Not all dangerous plants grow in the field; beware of over-hanging trees from neighbouring property which may be poisonous. Delightful-looking but deadly is laburnum, beloved of gardeners. Churchyards invariably are home to the yew. Prior to the enclosures of the Middle Ages and the eighteenth and nineteenth centuries, when open areas were fenced, the churchyard was unusual in being securely fenced, so was a safe place to grow this valuable timber. Over-hanging yew trees present a considerable risk to stock grazing a neighbouring field, as all parts of the tree are poisonous, although not usually eaten unless cut and wilted. Yew is a swift and fatal poison.

Broom — colourful, unpalatable, but poisonous.

Privet bush in a garden hedge — poisonous!

Churchyard yew — a deadly poison.

Colourful laburnum is a deadly poison. It is grown mainly in gardens.

Once it is certain that there are no dangerous plants, or if there were they have all been pulled up by the roots, removed and completely burnt or safely disposed of, then the horses can be removed while topping is carried out, and replaced afterwards to eat up the toppings. Deep-rooted 'herbs' (weeds!)

Herb-rich hedge sides give variety and interest to grazing as well as providing a greater range of vitamins and minerals. Heavy applications of fertiliser destroy these colourful plants.

Bright and beautiful, lords-and-ladies is also known as cuckoo pint and wild arum lily. The berries are more dangerous to small children than to horses.

When the grazing is as short as this, and the piles of droppings numerous and obvious, harrowing and resting the field is the only option.

will have benefited from minerals deeper in the soil than shallow-rooting grass can obtain. Nettles in particular are high in minerals, almost to the same extent as seaweed, and with the same benefits. Country people appreciate the value of nettles (which are not touched by livestock when they are growing) and have used them as a remedy for laminitis. Medicinally beneficial or not, these wilted weeds provide some extra food which the horses enjoy. Once cleared of its weedy opposition, grass will be able to recover more easily. If topping is repeated as soon as the weeds are becoming obvious again, it will soon be clear that each time there is less to cut.

Grass thrives on being cut and grazed. Its growing point is near the ground, so unless grazing is allowed to continue to the point where the grass is down to the roots, the plant itself is not damaged. In fact, it is encouraged. Other herbaceous plants (weeds again!) have their vital growing point at the top of the plant, so cutting (or grazing) is far more damaging. If topping is repeated as often as necessary and before the plant has a chance to go to seed, it will eventually be killed off.

If you are unsure of being able to make an accurate identification of poisonous plants, or are not absolutely certain that there is no chance of poisonous plants being amongst the toppings, then do not take the risk of allowing horses to graze them.

Toppings, free of poisonous plants of course, are usually safe for horses to eat, unlike lawn mowings. Lawn mowings are finely cut, and are usually from short, green grass which is young and sweet. Collected into heaps or bags, the mowings quickly ferment, the sugars from the grass forming gas and toxins which are harmful to horses. They can cause a nasty, even fatal, colic. Toppings are much coarser, being generally composed of fibrous weeds and seeding grasses. The sugar content is low, fermentation much less likely, and so the risk is a lot less. However, if, due to low stocking rates, for instance, the areas to be topped are thick, lush or extensive, it may be advisable to stagger the topping over a few days so that the horses cannot gorge themselves.

Once the toppings have been eaten, or not, if you have decided it could be too risky, the horses should be brought in, wormed and put on to another paddock. The grazed field can then be harrowed using a chain harrow. This distributes the dung, pulls out matted grass and can also help to smooth out rough or poached areas. It needs to be fairly dry for harrowing, or the operation will damage the field, leaving tractor tracks and a lot of mud. Harrowing is good for grass and is also discouraging to weeds. By spreading the dung, it helps to prevent 'roughs' getting established and helps to fertilise the field. However, by spreading the droppings, it is also spreading any worm eggs or larvae that might be in them. For this reason, it is best to harrow on a dry sunny day as desiccation kills worms. Immature worms are sometimes able to survive the frosts of winter, but they are always vulnerable to the drying effects of strong sun accompanied by a breeze.

These wide grass harrows fold up to go through gateways. Note the well-broken and dispersed dung piles.

The pasture should not be grazed for at least three weeks. After three weeks, most of the residual redworm eggs (strongyles) will have hatched out into larvae, and in this time most of the larvae will have perished for want of an equine host. The eggs of the roundworm (ascarids), however, are not so vulnerable and can survive for up to five years. If harrowing is a part of the equine pasture management, it can only be successful in conjunction with an effective and thorough worming programme. If this is the case, then harrowing is a most valuable contributor to keeping the pasture in good condition. In fact, by preventing the build-up of matted grass and by aerating the turf, it is making conditions less favourable for the small forage mite which is the alternative host to the horse tapeworm, increasingly recognised as a problem to many horses and especially to those grazing old, upland, tussocky or unmanaged grassland.

During the summer sojourn at grass, your youngster will still need plenty of care. Vaccinations should be kept up to date and it should be brought in for the farrier to trim the feet. Most youngsters easily go twelve weeks between trims but if the feet or limbs are not absolutely straight it is better to get the farrier in every six weeks, or as frequently as (s)he advises.

After a winter of over-use or perhaps just due to old age and neglect, the grass can become worn out and unproductive. It is tempting to consider ploughing and reseeding, but with horses this is best avoided. Horses exercise far more at grass than other animals and their hooves cut up the turf. Once this happens, the structure of the turf and upper layers of soil are damaged and the ground becomes poached — a wet and muddy morass that is useless, unsightly and difficult to walk in. Ploughing obviously gets rid of any turf that may remain and for the first season at least after reseeding the ground will be bare between the new tufts of grass. This will poach very quickly. It is better to preserve and encourage whatever turf there is. Small damaged areas can be reseeded by hand, broadcasting a mixture of soil and seed any time during the spring through to late summer. For larger areas, techniques such as slot seeding are very good. A special drill plants the seed in small slots cut into the existing turf. This operation is carried out by a contractor, using the seed mix of your choice. It is recommended that following the drilling, the field is grazed right down tight to remove the competition of the existing grass, then rested to allow the new grass to grow. There is minimum disruption, the field is out of commission for only a matter of weeks and it is economical.

Rye grass in the centre, timothy grass on the right of the picture; both are good, nutritious grasses for horses.

The choice of grass seed needs consideration. Some seed companies have studied the needs of horses carefully and produced excellent mixtures. The grasses must be palatable, so it is best, for instance, to avoid cocksfoot. This is a productive and nourishing grass, but quickly becomes tough, when the horses will not touch it. It establishes easily in the 'rough' dunged areas. As horses are such notorious poachers, grasses which form a dense, close turf, covering all the soil with fine but resiliant grass are to be included in a horse paddock mix. Such grasses are crested dog's tail (which they relish as well) and creeping red fescue. Timothy grass is a useful addition to the mix, as it grows late into the autumn, providing some keep when many other grasses have ceased growing. Meadow fescue and meadow foxtail are also good, and grow early in the season. Various types of rye grass will make up the bulk of the mixtures, but the genetically engineered tetraploid rye grasses should be avoided as these have been shown to cause laminitis in horses. They produce high levels of carbohydrates, which are not well tolerated by horses. The inclusion of a few herbs adds variety and interest. A little clover, chicory and yarrow for instance will add colour and interest as well. Chicory has delightful bright blue flowers, the yarrow dense heads of tiny white and pink flowers.

Yarrow as seen here can be pink or white; it is a useful herb of old meadows, enjoyed by horses and with the reputation for being valuable in treating colds, headaches and fevers.

Good grazing will only occur on good soil. For the soil to remain healthy, it must normally be drained, and the drains and ditches will need maintaining. Establishing new drainage is expensive and professional advice from a drainage contractor should be sought. Certain areas, such as water meadows, may be protected, in which case you may not be allowed to drain them. If this is the case, you will usually be given advice and guidance on the management of these protected meadows by the authority controlling them, such as the Countryside Commission.

Grazing by all animals, but especially horses, can make the soil acidic. This makes clay soils heavier and reduces further their ability to drain. It will be noticed that under such conditions, buttercups, for example, become increasingly obvious. These are not grazed, so thrive. Topping will help to control them, but unless the soil conditions are altered to be more desirable to good grasses and less conducive to buttercups, the problem will continue. Acid soils are deficient in calcium, a major mineral component of bones, so of vital importance to growing horses. As the soil becomes increasingly acid, more and more undesirable and less nutritious grasses and herbs will grow, less of the 'good' grass will flourish and the ability of the grazing to provide sufficient nutrition and minerals will decline.

Acidity is measured by pH. Low numbers are acid: high numbers, alkaline, and pH 7 represents neutrality. At pH 6—6.5 the soil will provide the right conditions for the best grass and sufficient minerals for grazing horses. When the pH drops below 6, then measures must be taken to correct it, using some form of liming agent. Lime, or calcium carbonate, is most readily available as chalk, limestone or calcified seaweed (actually a form of coral). The plants growing (or not) on a pasture will you give the first indication of whether liming is needed.

Buttercups, with their gaudy yellow flowers, will be increasingly obvious, but clover and its relations will be missing from the sward. The leguminous plants all require plenty of calcium in the soil, and in return, supply it to the grazing stock in their leaves, flowers and stems. A garden soil test kit will give a guide to pH, but very often the contractors supplying the liming agent will operate a free soil pH testing service.

Generally, liming has to be done by a contractor. Amounts of three tons of ground chalk per acre are beyond most individuals to spread! Once it is done, liming on this scale should last for around eight years. If the form of chalk applied is 'one inch screed to dust' the dust is available immediately; the larger lumps of chalk (up to 1 in. or 2.5 cm) take longer to break down, giving a timed release of the lime over the years. The grazing can be used again three weeks after application or after sufficient rain has fallen to wash the chalk dust off the grass.

An alternative, which is also suitable for small areas, is the calcified seaweed. This is dredged up from the relatively warm coastal waters off the south-west coast of England and Brittany in France, where the effects of the North Atlantic

Drift (part of the Gulf Stream) create unexpectedly mild conditions, in which the coral thrives. It comes in small lumps (from 1 cm to the size of a pin-head) in 50 kg bags. Five bags per acre will not only provide lime, but also offer many other trace elements as well. Being an organic product, it also encourages soil bacteria to multiply and grass to root deeper. In practice, the grass grows later into the autumn, is more drought resistant and there is a less marked 'spring flush'. Calcified seaweed can be applied by hand (wear leather or rubber gloves as it can be abrasive) or with a tractor-mounted fertiliser spinner, such as one used for spreading granular fertiliser, on a wide setting. The effects will last for at least three years. Calcified seaweed can be applied at any time. There is no need to remove the horses or to rest the paddocks after applying it.

If the pasture was in good condition before the grazing started, liming and harrowing in droppings should maintain it in good order for grazing, for the majority of what is taken by the horses is recycled as droppings. If a hay crop is taken, then obviously the pasture has suffered a net loss, which will need to be made good with fertiliser.

Nitrogenous fertilisers applied in the spring enhance the spring flush of grass. If the grass is being taken for hay in June or July this is not a problem. But for grazing horses, already at risk of laminitis from spring grass, the consequences of grazing grass top-dressed with nitrogen can be disastrous. Also, such an enhanced early growth will inevitably reduce the grass's ability to remain productive for so long into the autumn. For grazing, nitrogenous, spring-applied fertilisers should not be used. Organic, slow release fertilisers which are usually applied in the autumn or even winter are more appropriate. Farmyard manure is very suitable when it is felt that fertiliser is required. Well-rotted stable muck can also be acceptable. In some areas, treated sewage sludge is available, but it is important that the sludge and the soil are regularly tested for the presence of toxic heavy metals such as lead and mercury. The risk of these is higher in industrial locations.

Pig manure is generally not advisable as it is rather rank and encourages the growth of weeds. Chicken manure should

Hay-making in the north of England is never easy; high rainfall and a colder climate are not conducive to good hay. This hay turner creates a high windrow to accelerate the drying process.

never be used as it is too strong and is deficient in copper. Copper is a trace element without which the horse could become anaemic. It is also believed that copper deficiency may result in pigment loss from the skin, and ultimately the hair, in spots around the eyes, muzzle and even the whole body. Horses grazed on land fertilised with poultry muck are more likely to develop laminitis.

8 CARE OF THE YOUNGSTER AT GRASS

Whilst at grass, visit your young horse twice a day. It is not necessary or even advisable to catch it every time, for if you do so, it may decide it is not to its liking and refuse to be caught at all. When you do catch it, however, always give a reward of a few horse and pony nuts or a carrot, preferably from a bucket. It is important that it realises food comes from a bucket (or manger) and not directly from yourself. Feeding from the hand can result in the horse nipping, biting or even kicking when you do not have a tit-bit.

Some visits to the horse may be just a quick glance to make sure that all is right; on others, you may lead it around a little, perhaps brush out the mane if it is getting tangled, or, if you have someone with you to hold it, pick out the feet. Thus it will not forget what was learnt over the winter, but neither will you be off-putting by making your presence associated with being disciplined all the time. Basically, these are social visits, enjoyable for both of you.

On your routine, twice daily visits, check the fencing, water and make sure grazing is sufficient. Once a week, have a thorough inspection of the fences, repairing, renailing, creosoting and tensioning as required. Major problems will, of course, need attention as soon as they occur. Also make sure your security arrangements are satisfactory. Gates will need padlocking or otherwise securing at the hinge end as well as the latch end. Befriend neighbours who can 'keep an eye' during your absence. Committed horse thieves will break fences, drop ramps across ditches and sometimes lead horses considerable distances to avoid raising suspicion. It is worth

Elizabeth gives Shiny a check over, but today does not catch her.

(*Opposite*) Yearling fillies recently turned out in early autumn. This field has not been grazed or managed all season, and the grass is long and apparently dead. It will provide almost limitless amounts of fibre, but will be of low feed value. This can easily be made up with two small feeds a day. The belt of woodland offers excellent, natural shelter from the north.

Safe post and rail fencing, a stout, well-hung gate, a wide access track and a shelter belt of trees — a wonderful environment for horses, but expensive to maintain.

considering extra ways of reducing the chances of theft. Freeze-branding leaves visible marks which are an obvious deterrent and also easily spotted by the police and others who may be handling or looking for misplaced horses. If rugs are used which cover the area marked, copy the brand on to the rug to draw attention to the fact that the horse is marked. Grey horses, however dark as youngsters, and some are almost black, all lighten over the years, so when getting these branded, make sure that the iron is left on long enough to kill the hair totally in order to bald-brand. Normal freeze-brands leave white marks which will, of course become invisible as a grey horse ages and the coat whitens.

Personally, I do not like the practice of freeze-branding on the saddle area. Firstly it is too often covered up, either by tack or rugs, removing some of the deterrent value. Secondly, the saddle area is already very vulnerable, bearing the saddle and the rider's weight as it does. To compromise this area further with a brand seems unwise. The bald branding necessary on greys must particularly increase the risk of saddle sores, especially if the horse is intended for prolonged exercise, such as endurance riding. In the winter the brand on any horse is only clearly legible if the area is clipped. Clipping the saddle area should never be considered, as it vastly increases the risk of saddle sores or the stubble wearing away to leave totally

Kadir and the yearlings enjoying some fun.

bald and so very vulnerable patches. Other sites which can be freeze-marked include the shoulder, neck or hindquarters. Obviously a brand on the neck, opposite the fall of the mane, is most visible, least likely to be covered and at no risk of galling. Freeze brands which leave the skin pink are at risk of becoming photosensitised when exposed to sun.

Other identification techniques include the insertion of microchips, which is excellent provided the police, for instance, have a suitable scanner or detector to 'read' the horse, but it is not as clearly obvious as a freeze-brand. An identifying mark, such as one's post code, can be branded on to the feet, half on one fore foot and half on the other, and similarly on the hind feet as the brands on the fore feet are growing out, so there is always a clearly visible mark. This is very quick, totally painless (unlike freeze-branding, which although not initially painful is extremely painful in the days following branding) and relatively cheap. It is not so obvious if the feet are muddy and needs reapplying every four to six months.

Permanent marks should be undertaken before turning out for the summer and, in the case of branding, three weeks allowed for them to heal, as flies will be attracted to the area after branding until it has healed over.

As a further precaution, it is wise to have some good photographs of your horse. A clear picture from each side,

Kadir has been freeze-marked on his neck, which may be a preferred site to the saddle area. The neck is not covered by rugs, nor subject to the stresses imposed by the saddle.

Chrysanda (one year) posing nicely for a snap at only her second show — results were disappointing as she has 'gone up behind'. It will be several months before she is looking her level best again.

plus a head-on shot to show any face markings, should provide a good identification. Keep the photographs and the negatives, should you need to have copies made, in a safe place along with the horse's registration documents, freeze-brand certificate, and vaccination record. Roans are often a different colour in the winter, and some palominos, although dark gold in July, may be white in winter, so if yours is a horse which changes colour have a summer set of photographs and a winter set. Greys, which change colour with each coat change until they are white or flea-bitten grey, should be re-photographed twice a year until the coat has ceased to change colour.

It is likely that one of the first things to happen to your youngster after turning out is that it will put on a spurt of growth. This is normal, nature's way of making the most of the grass when it is at its most nutritious. What is, however, a bit alarming is the way in which they grow, for it is quite common for the hindquarters to grow first. This makes the horse 'up behind' and in fact it can be even two or three inches higher in the croup than at the withers. When putting on height, it is unlikely that the youngster will gain weight as well, so it may look a bit plain. This does not matter so long

as it is obvious that the horse is basically well — alert, lively and with a good coat. It is better for growth if the youngster is not fat; overweight thoroughbred yearlings produced for the autumn sales are often noticed to increase their height as the fat is shed when they start training for racing.

It is at this time that a pretty youngster can start turning into an ugly duckling. Being up behind makes the shoulder appear straight and shortens the stride. The horse becomes unbalanced with more weight than usual on the forehand. But do not despair, as the former good looks will return when it levels up later in the season.

During the summer, shelter from the hottest sun and the flies will be appreciated. Natural shelter provided by a tall hedge or mature trees will be used more readily than, say, a shed-type shelter, but even this is better than no shelter.

As further protection from flies, long-acting pyrethrum-based fly repellents are very good. A ready-to-use version can be purchased from saddleries, or the concentrate for home-mixing can be obtained from your veterinary surgeon. The instructions on the pack should be followed carefully, especially concerning dilution rates, use of protective gloves and safe disposal of empty containers and unused product. It can be

(*Left*) In the summer, when young horses have been out all night, coming in to a cool stable can be very welcome. Here, yearling Jenerous makes the most of a soft straw bed on a sweltering day in June.

(*Right*) An oak tree on the brook's bank provides welcome shade for yearling Trickery and two-year-old Cruise. If autumn grazing is sparse, take measures to avoid horses eating acorns from oak trees, as they are poisonous: either keep the horses out of the field, collect or — if the ground is damp — roll the acorns in. If hay is provided, the horses are less likely to be hungry and so less likely to consume acorns.

Blue has managed to graze her hip. No real damage was done, and the hair has regrown with the help of a soothing ointment and fly repellent. Greys and roans, as here, often require a further coat change to achieve a perfect match!

applied with a spray or simply swabbed on with a sponge. Pay particular attention to the head, but be very careful not to get it in the eyes, ears, nostrils or mouth. The legs should also be thoroughly treated, as the horse fly selects the legs especially for laying its bot eggs. One application lasts from two weeks to four weeks. If the flies are bad, it may be necessary to 'top up' round the eyes on a daily basis, using a roll-on repellent, which is accurate and non-run. Some horses have very sensitive skin and may become allergic to certain fly repellants. The skin becomes raised, causing the hair to stand out. If the repellant was applied in stripes, then the raised areas of the reaction will appear along the same stripes. If this occurs, the repellant should be washed off with horse shampoo, and a note made of the product which caused the reaction so that its future use can be avoided.

Playful, inquisitive youngsters will, almost inevitably, collect the odd cut or scrape from time to time. Unless these need the vet (see later chapter) they are easily treated, but should not be neglected, because flies and contamination can turn a simple graze into an infected open sore. An antiseptic wipe (or several) of the type sold in chemists for use in, say, travelling first aid kits, will clean up small injuries which can then be dressed with antiseptic cream or powder. Near a joint, cream is preferable as powder can form a dry scab which will break with movement.

Encircle the injury with a wipe from the roll-on fly repellent to keep the flies and their germs away. Some wound powders contain their own fly repellent, but there is no harm in using some more to be on the safe side. There are now available wax-based sticks containing both antiseptic and fly repellent. These can be wiped directly across minor injuries, are quick, effective and do not sting.

Aerosols are not advisable. The antiseptic content is usually carried in a spirit base. Although very effective, these treat-ments are very painful as they sting on contact with the wound. The noise of an aerosol is swiftly associated with the pain of the spirit on an open wound, which can make the horse for ever nervous of all aerosols, whether or not future ones cause pain. A nervous horse is difficult to treat and a difficult horse is a danger to its handler, so it is a scenario best avoided. Use non-painful treatments whenever you can. Creams and ointments are generally soothing, not stinging.

Surface injuries should be dry and healing well within a day or two of initiating appropriate treatment.

As summer progresses into autumn, the yearling will be levelling up, that is, the height at the withers gradually matching the height at the croup. Most of its growing is now done; over the next two or three years, it may grow another 2½ inches (5 cm) or so. Its appearance is more gawky and a bit gangly, compared with a mature horse, but no longer babyish. It will start to make a winter coat when the nights get chillier in August. At first, it will be just a bit fluffier than the summer coat, then as the frosts start and autumn holds a clearer promise of winter to come, the coat will get longer.

A long, muddy winter coat provides good protection for this contented grass-kept two year old.

Rising two years old: Arab filly Kassya is relaxed and happy turned out on a late winter's morning.

As long as the horse is keeping well, it will do it good to stay out as long as possible, probably until Christmas and maybe even later if it is a dry winter. From about November, extra forage in the form of hay may be needed, up to half a bale per horse per day (10 kg). In very cold, or wet, weather, hard feed may also be necessary, up to 3 kg a day.

Shelter will be needed from driving rain but as long as it is not cold, wet and windy at the same time, it is unlikely that the horse will suffer if it has plenty of good hay to eat.

There are distinct advantages in keeping your yearling out as long as possible. It is of course natural and it is healthier, since in the open there are not the dust levels that occur in stables. So many horses seem to develop allergies to stable dust that it can only be sensible to keep them away from a potentially dusty environment whenever it is possible.

Work is not yet planned, so a thick coat is an advantage, not a handicap. The horse will grow a full winter coat, so if conditions deteriorate or if the ground gets very poached making stabling necessary, rugs can be avoided. Young horses are more likely to get rubbed by rugs, as they are not yet the standard, adult shape for which most rugs are cut. Some youngsters can be very heavy on rugs as they are liable to chew them, rub them on the walls and destroy them generally in any way they can. If you are showing (see later chapters), especially early season shows, you may feel rugging is essential, but be prepared for the expense of replacing torn and mangled rugs!

The winter coat may be long and shaggy; as well as providing warmth, it will acquire a layer of mud. The mud adds to the insulating effect, and prevents the coat from being disturbed in the wind which also helps to keep the horse warm. As mud can serve a useful purpose, do not feel that it is necessary to remove it with daily grooming.

Having the chance to develop a good coat and some winter hardiness while young will make future winters easier. Whilst it is not so important for a riding horse to get a good coat when in work, for it will probably be stabled, rugged and even clipped out anyway, there are plenty of occasions when it is better and more convenient for the horse to live out. The rider may be incapacitated or the horse may be lame, for instance. Several months at grass is often recommended to aid recovery following tendon injury. If the horse develops the ability to cope with the less-than-perfect conditions when younger, it will be more able to adapt later, and will in any case not feel the cold in bad weather as much as the horse who has all its life been protected against the elements.

Young colts wintering out in suitable surroundings. Their thick coats insulate them so well that the snow on their backs is unmelted.

9 AND INTO THE THIRD YEAR

Inevitably, the weather will deteriorate or the ground will poach to an unacceptable level, and the young horse will need to be brought in. Wintering out for the whole winter is really only a possibility on well-drained land in mild conditions and on very generous acreages. Two or three acres per horse will be needed to begin to avoid the ground poaching to an unacceptable level. Shelter will be needed. A shed or field shelter is rarely satisfactory, as the horses soon poach the area immediately in front of the shelter. Tall, thick hedges or even a belt of woodland is far more satisfactory. Not only does the wide area of shelter suffer less from poaching, but there is less risk of the horses injuring each other by kicking in the confined space of a field shelter. Further, a dominant horse does not have the same opportunity to deny a lower ranking one access to shelter.

By now, the horse is rising two years old. As a two year old, no longer a baby, the horse will be becoming more confident, stronger and able to cope more readily with change. New challenges will be met with more assurance and less wariness or fear. It is also a time when the horse may start challenging your authority, so it is important not to let it get the upper hand. Make sure that in the small but important ways the horse is acknowledging and submitting to your superiority. At a word, it should step back from the stable door to let you in, and wait while the food is put in the manger or the haynet is tied up. When grooming, always tie the horse up – this is a very simple but effective way of maintaining your authority and also of ensuring that you have

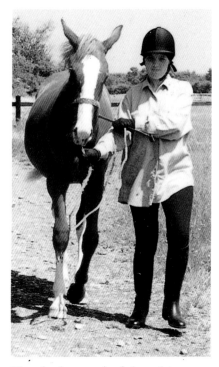

Use the butt end of the whip to push the youngster away if he is getting too close. Stud trainee, Jo, with yearling Anglo-Arab, Clyde. Note the handler and horse are in step, as they should be.

(*Opposite*) Even in blizzard conditions, horses appreciate some fresh air. Clearly, Merlin would rather be outside than in!

65

A good gallop for playful youngsters on a misty winter's morning.

the horse's undivided attention.

By the time it goes out to grass again as a two year old, lessons already learned can be refined and new ones taught.

When leading it is a good thing for the youngster to learn to walk or trot with a gap between itself and yourself. If it can learn to keep a metre or so between you, it is learning to become a little bit independent, is less likely to tread on you if it spooks, and when the time comes to start education for riding it will be much easier to lunge, having already discovered that it is not essential to have you close by all the time.

In these three pictures, we see how Olive successfully teaches Caramel to walk calmly, keeping a greater distance between horse and handler. Olive should wear gloves.

Three happy yearlings! Justinus (left) is a colt, the other two are geldings.

You may find that gradually increasing the distance from yourself to the horse is sufficient; another horse may close the gap as soon as you create it. If this happens, carry a whip or stout cane in your right hand and use the butt end against the shoulder or base of the neck as a prod to encourage the horse to keep the space between you. At all times, encourage the horse to walk freely forward with a light or even loose contact on the lead rope.

If it is sluggish, use a long whip (such as a schooling whip) in your left hand and flick this behind you on to the youngster's hindquarters to encourage it to walk on. At the same time, use a vocal command, '*walk on*'. Should the horse react too keenly, be sure not to punish it inadvertently by jabbing or jerking on your lead rein.

As a two year old, the horse will be ready to accept changes and challenges in its life. Planning a few shows, even if yours is not an obvious show horse, can be very beneficial as it educates the youngster to accept changes of environment, new sights and sounds, and can also help to strengthen the bond of leadership and friendship between you. It will give a purpose to leading lessons, grooming, and travelling practice, as well as being enjoyable. There is also the opportunity to compare your young horse with others of a similar age or type.

A group of friends get together at their livery yard to have a show, giving the youngsters (second and third from right) valuable experience. Diane, who has a nice hat, is roped in as 'judge'.

10 SHOWING

Your youngster can't do any work yet − no riding, lungeing, driving or even hauling logs, but one thing you can do together is showing.

If you are only interested in the result then showing really is the 'mug's game' we're so often being told it is! No two judges will ever get the same result, even with the same horses, same handlers and on the same day. But if showing is regarded as a good way of getting your youngster accustomed to travelling, behaving well in strange company, coping with new sights and sounds and remaining compliant even in trying circumstances, then whatever the result of the judging you will be a winner every time.

There is no point in showing if you don't try to do it properly. A lot of effort goes into producing a well-trained show horse. If you take it out before it is ready or with insufficient preparation, the chances are that neither of you will enjoy the occasion and instead of benefiting, the poor horse may be so confused and bewildered that it could end up mistrusting all future attempts at travelling or any bustle that might be associated with a show.

Showing should not be taken so seriously that the horse's best interests are compromised. Fortunately, one sees fewer overweight show horses today, but there are still some which resemble fat stock more than young stock. Overloading young limbs increases the likelihood of arthritic conditions developing, of strained tendons and misaligned limbs. Even the action will suffer − overweight juveniles are more likely to be short striding in adulthood, or even develop dishing in their action. When the ground is hard, extra weight in the body leads to extra concussion on the feet and limbs in trot, making the development of navicular disease more likely (see Chapter 11).

So even show horses should be fit as well as being sufficiently 'furnished' to look good; they need plenty of exercise and, of course, company. You may feel that being out at grass in a large group, whilst natural, may increase the risk of lumps and bumps from fun and games and that all that good grazing leads to a grass belly, but even if your show horse lives in at night, the benefits of spending a large part of the day turned out should not be sacrificed. The best fencing and fewer and quieter companions are a reasonable option for the duration of a short showing season.

Campaigning an inexperienced horse round lots of shows all season risks making it bored, miserable or just unhappy. In a dry summer, trotting out on hard ground risks damage to the joints and bones of the limbs. It is better to aim for a few shows one or two weeks apart over, say, two months, at the end of which time it can revert to normality, having done enough to learn from experience but not having overdone it to the point of detriment.

The procedure for showing is fairly straightforward and much the same for all British breeds and types, with minor variations to enhance particular characteristics of distinctive types. The technique is a different matter! In the standard British method, exhibits are led around the ring in walk on the right rein, so the handlers are on the far side from the judge. Before the judge (via the steward) forms the preliminary line up, each exhibit may trot in turn round the ring to join the other end of the queue — a bit like the 'trot to the rear' in the riding school! The judge can see only the side view, so it is often taken as a good opportunity to show off the horse's length of stride.

Once each exhibit has trotted, the whole class will be asked by the steward to walk round again. Leave several horses' lengths in front of you after the person before you has walked on; your horse will stand out favourably if it has a little space around it. It also gives you scope to walk out freely, especially

Two-year-old Anglo–Arab colt, Scindian Chieftain, in good order for showing. Although stabled, he has six hours at grass every day and three times a week is walked out for forty-five minutes. This is a good compromise and ensures that he is content as well as looking good.

if your exhibit has a good long stride. This is the time the judge is making the initial choice, so it is important to make the most of all opportunities to set up your horse favourably. The steward, in response to the judge's bidding, will line the class up, facing the spectators. It is appropriate to keep an attentive eye on the steward all the time, for it is (s)he who is in charge of directing all the proceedings in the ring. At this time especially, be ready to respond immediately to any signal. (S)he may point at you, call the colour of your horse or raise his bowler hat to you. It will help the smooth running of the class if you position yourself so that you can see the steward. With a small horse you will be able to watch the steward over the horse's back; with a larger horse you may have to peer under its neck, especially if you are short. Either way, ensure you do not miss your signal to come into line.

As you come into line, turn to face the horse, so you can see that it halts correctly. Remain facing it, partly to keep it standing well, but partly to enable spectators to see the number on your back, which they can check against the details in the catalogue.

Standing in this position, you can also see what is going on behind the horse. It is wise to adopt this stance whenever your horse is standing in company or if there are people and especially children around. Young horses can be very quick to

Worth the hard work! Justinus is second at his first show as a two year old.

Running in step with your horse is actually easier than it looks, but needs practice! Jackie and Justinus showing how it should be done.

kick out if they sense anything behind them. Later, they will have learned from your tutelage not to kick, but until then, keeping an eye on the horse's hindquarters can give the opportunity to take swift evasive action should a horse or a toddler come within range of a possible kick. A well-fed, healthy young animal surrounded by strange sights and sounds and possibly attracting the attention of spectators in the ring and elsewhere in the showground is always a potential danger. However quiet or good at home, take every precaution at shows to protect the public and other horses from risk of injury, or indeed your own horse from being kicked by another.

Once lined up, each exhibit in turn comes out and stands up before the judge, who will examine the horse from the side, front, other side and rear view before you walk to the end of the ring (or a point designated by the steward) and then turn the horse about in its tracks to the right and return in trot. Thus the judge sees the walk from behind and the trot from in front as you run towards her, and from behind as you go past. If she's still looking, keep going right round the ring so she can have another side view!

Your own legs should move in unison with the horse's legs. By gradually lengthening your own stride as you trot, it is possible to encourage the horse to lengthen, too. By going in step with the horse you are creating a unity of purpose and

Well in step as a result of practice.
But don't practise too much –
two-year-old Shady looks rather
fed up!

it is possible this will encourage the youngster. It is also less
distracting for the judge. The handler running or walking out
of step with the horse creates an impression of a shorter,
choppier stride and the odd illusion of a horse with six legs.
With a little practice it will become second nature always to
be in step with your equine partner.

Turning the horse should always be to the right, so the
horse turns in a smaller circle, the handler walking round the
horse. This keeps good control of the hindquarters, which
then cannot swing out, it is safer, and returns the horse on the
same line, so the judge does not have to move far to view the
front having watched the hind view as the horse walked
away.

(*Left*) Turn the head first, and the
horse will follow.
(*Centre*) Tap the horse with the
whip behind you to encourage it to
walk on.
(*Right*) Pointing the whip across
the front of the horse helps him to
get the idea of turning to the right
(Louise and Biggles).

The horse may find turning to the right awkward at first. Practice at home will ensure that you and your horse are comfortable with this manoeuvre.

After each exhibit has been examined in this way, all are usually asked to walk round again before the final order is called. Your position is only confirmed when the rosettes have been handed out.

Walking round the ring for standard British breeds is done to the right (clockwise) with the handler on the nearside of the horse. Thus the judge has an uninterrupted view of the horse. American breeds go counterclockwise and some European breeds are shown individually on a triangle.

Much of what is required in the ring is useful at other times in our young horse's career. Walking quietly and well in-hand makes turning out and fetching in easier; it is also a good way of taking exercise together, and should the horse unfortunately be injured, it may even be the only exercise suitable. Learning to stand well is helpful if you are trying to sell the horse or even just taking a decent photograph of him for your album. Trotting in a straight line on a free rein is a vital part of the veterinary examination for the suitability of a horse at purchase or just checking if it is sound, following farriery, for instance. You will be glad it learned to stand obediently, ignoring the sights and sounds of a show, when it hacks out for the first time on the roads. Waiting at road junctions is no problem for a horse accustomed to waiting around at horse shows!

Finally, accustoming it to travelling whilst still young creates good habits that will hopefully remain with the horse for ever (see Chapter 13).

Before showing, allow plenty of time — time to assess good and bad points and make plans to enhance the former and diminish the latter. Allow time to condition your horse. It will need to be the right weight, fit enough, with a shining coat, feet trimmed and level and if a breed or type that is shown plaited, you will need to allow plenty of time for mane pulling and trimming. Teaching it to lead well, trot straight and true, and pose like a professional will all take time, too.

If you are planning on exhibiting at early shows — April and May — more preparation time is needed so that you can get rid of the winter woollies in time for your horse to look its best. It will, almost certainly, involve rugging from New Year onwards, having brought him in at least at night from around the end of October. In fact rugging from October can even prevent such a heavy coat from growing in the first place.

The winter coat is shed in response to the improved diet, increased day length, and warmer weather that spring brings

Jamborino (one year) is obviously well — he looks fit and alert and his coat is shining. For showing he would need just a little more condition, especially on his neck.

Two-year-old Anglo-Arab filly practises looking pretty at home in a show bridle.

Teaching your horses to stand up at home for photographs gives you a good idea of how to make them look their best for the show ring. Caramel's head could be a bit lower, and Shiny's near fore should be back and her off fore forward.

naturally. If this is unlikely to have occurred in time for early shows, nature can be helped along with a little encouragement. Although rugged and stabled horses may develop less winter coat, that which they do have can be shed later, probably due to the fact that stabling reduces their effective day length.

Stabling and rugging will create warmer conditions for the horse. Leaving the stable lights on until your bedtime or final check round can effectively increase the day length. Feeding is not always effective if it involves solely increasing the levels of basic hard feeds. Spring grass is green and naturally high in carotene, the precursor of vitamin A, one of the so-called sunshine vitamins. Using a feed similar to spring grass is more efficacious than cereal based feeds. Dried lucerne (alfalfa), conveniently fed in pelletted form, is an ideal way of meeting this need. The addition of cod liver oil, sunflower or any other good quality vegetable oil to the feed can also help hasten the coat change. Feed one to two tablespoonfuls daily (15−30 ml) depending on the size of the horse.

Daily grooming removes the old coat as soon as it loosens and helps further by increasing the circulation of blood in the deeper layers of the skin. Oil from the sebaceous glands is distributed along the hair shaft with thorough grooming and strapping, which enhances the appearance of the coat.

Mid season shows, in June and July, are probably the easiest to prepare for. The preparations should not be started later than six weeks before the first show, however, especially if the horse is out of condition, needs a lot of attention to his feet or has not had a lot of handling.

Bringing a horse out later in the season, August and September, may give you a competitive edge over rivals which have become bored, but the ground is often hard, flies are worse and you will have to stable at nights in August to delay the onset of the winter coat. Many of the affiliated shows will already have taken place, especially those running Horse of the Year Show qualifiers, so your choice at this end of the season may be a bit limited to smaller affiliated shows and club shows.

If you are a serious competitor, then you will do the whole season, hopefully finishing up with the Horse of the Year

Show in October. You will keep your young horse stabled, rugged, corn fed and limit his exercise. Time out will increase the risk of injury; he may charge around and get splints or get bitten or kicked by companions. In any case, it could rob him of energy and exuberance, all of which he will need in the ring in order to look good. Right? The sad facts are that many horses subjected to this regime fail to make the grade as riding horses. Their legs are overworked, their minds distorted, their bodies bloated and their constitutions softened by the artificial, pampered life style. As your young horse is a riding horse waiting to develop, avoid any temptation to risk robbing him of his future by over-producing him for the show ring.

Visit some shows on foot before venturing out with your own horse if you have never shown before. This will enable you to become familiar with the procedure and pick up some tips on technique.

Leading should not be a problem for a well-brought-up young horse, but for the ring, it looks better if you can walk a little further away from him than usual. Gradually do this at home, using the fat end of a longish whip as a prod on his

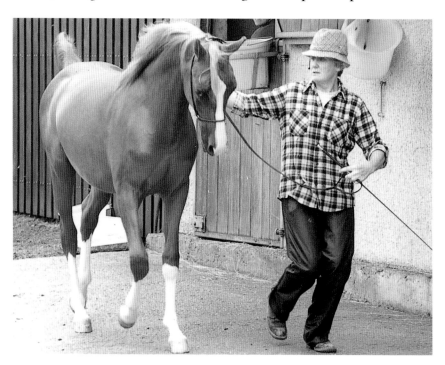

Showing off to visitors at home is an excellent part of the preparation of young horses for the show ring. Arab colt Tibre showing his paces at Al Waha Stud.

neck or shoulder to explain what is required if necessary. Never, ever hit a horse unless he has shown violence towards you. Unnecessary use of a whip, where it is not warranted and probably not understood by the unfortunate victim, will serve only to make the horse more difficult in the future, especially colts. Fear makes horses unpredictable but if your violence initiates a similar reaction back, you can only lose; a two-year-old colt, for instance, flexing his muscles is an extremely strong and potentially dangerous creature. Correction where it is deserved, however, is a different matter, provided the horse understands why it has been hit.

Encourage it to walk straight, with the head and neck in line with the body. If it has a good walk, with a long, ground-devouring stride, you will have to get a move on yourself! Try to walk in step, for the reasons mentioned above.

The trot, too, should be presented with you discreetly in control, a metre or so away from the horse. Use your voice to encourage him to trot − remember that horses have a good sense of hearing, so it is not necessary to shout. Back up with a tickle from your long whip held in your left hand if it does not understand. But before becoming too dependent on your schooling whip, check your show rules − many have restrictions on the length of whip allowed. You may handle yours correctly, with kindness, and fairly, but others have not. Some shows limit the whip to 1 metre, others to 30 inches. Check first and school accordingly.

Shiny starts her training for trotting in hand while out in familiar surroundings. Olive keeps the pace steady and the distance short.

Avoid the temptation to start your run before the horse! Break into a run after it has started to trot. Otherwise, it will soon learn that if it lets you go first, there is little you can do to make it trot if it decides walking is less effort and more relaxing! In any case, pulling the horse from the front is more likely to result in its pulling back against you, with the head up and ears back, than producing a good trot.

Always start your trot slowly and calmly. Speed is not required when the judge is looking directly from the front or rear. It is more important to keep straight and let the judge see that your horse is in fact a perfect mover. Once out around the ring, it is possible to extend and show the judge (and everyone else) the true extent of your horse's magnificent action. If you have started calmly and increased the pace gradually, your horse should not break gait into canter. Canter is not required in-hand and, should your horse canter, immediately slow down, re-establish trot and try again to show extension without breaking. If breaking gait is a problem, you are probably asking too much, too soon, your horse is over excited or just plain cannot extend that much and canters in order to keep up with the handler. It may also be a warning that there is a discomfort in the feet. (See the section on navicular disease in Chapter 11.)

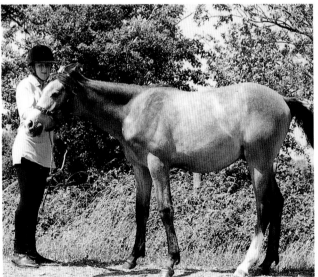

Even posing at home for a snap for the family album, it is worth getting the horse's attention and standing him well. Partbred Arab yearling, Biggles, looks three times the horse when Louise stands him up better!

Teaching your horse to stand correctly, calmly but with presence requires tact and patience but is well worth the effort, even if neither of you ever sees a show ring.

The absolutely four square halt does not always give the best impression when a horse is being viewed from the side. It gives the weird suggestion that the horse is in fact balanced on two legs. In practically every British breed or type, the legs will be arranged in the same way for showing, photography or even portrait painting. The diagonal legs (usually near fore and off hind — most photos are taken from the near side and most judges start by looking at that side) will be standing perpendicular, that is, with the cannon bones absolutely vertical. This may mean that the near fore is actually further forward than is normal for the horse, as many horses stand with their fore legs slightly behind the perpendicular. The off fore will be slightly back, just sufficient to show both the fore

At first, it is sufficient to practise in a headcollar. Posing for photographs is good experience for the horse and the handler. Three-year-old purebred Arab.

legs. Apart from revealing that the horse is normal rather than being an equine equivalent of a Reliant Robin, the shoulder is given a nice, sloping angle and the tricep muscle is held away from the girth line, avoiding the appearance of the horse looking tied-in at the elbow. Similarly, the nearside hind leg will be slightly back from its pair. This enhances the length of the hindquarter and especially the length from point of hip to point of hock. It avoids the horse looking sickle hocked and, from behind, avoids drawing attention to cow hocks.

Overall, the stance creates the impression that your horse stands over plenty of ground (the nearside legs being out slightly) but without being long in the back (the offside legs are 'square'). The position of the horse's head and neck varies with breed or type; generally, the neck should be slightly arched and extended forward to create the impression of a good length of rein. The promise of a small reward for good behaviour (a horse nut or pieces of grass but not sugar or mints − sweeties are even more likely to make your youngster greedy, grasping and nippy) will encourage an alert expression with the ears pointed forward.

In breeds with a history of driving and specific harness breeds, the stance for showing is somewhat different. In these cases, they are shown 'stretched', that is with the fore legs together and extended forward and the hind legs together and extended well out behind the horse. It is a very artificial pose, rendering the top line completely flat, raising a low-set tail, disguising the true angle of the hocks and could be construed as an exhibitor's way of hiding all known faults! In fact its origins are practical. Carriage horses were stood this way to make a speedy departure more difficult whilst the passengers were safely installed on board. Before moving off, the horses had to reposition themselves, so it was a sort of safety parking brake! Many of the horses shown stretched out this way will never know shafts, but in driving classes, especially for Hackneys, which are high-couraged, you will see the stance being used for its correct purpose. Welsh Cobs, a breed noted for its ground-devouring trot in harness, are also shown stretched or 'camped out', as are some of the American breeds. Certain other foreign breeds are stood square, so it is important

A Welsh Cob being shown in the traditional 'stretched' position.

to find out what is expected for your particular breed.

Teach your horse first of all to stand with his feet in the correct place. Watch them as you halt and try to establish the halt correctly from the walk. Aim to walk forward into the halt, but if your horse shuffles or creeps forward, tell it to get back and push it back to the original place, maintaining your position and authority. If you do not do this, you will find that it discovers it is amusing to creep forward and watch you retreat backwards. It is also encouraging the horse to crowd the handler, can contribute towards its becoming bargy, and is dangerous with colts, which may take it further by striking at the handler or knocking him or her over. At the show, you could find yourself constantly walking small circles to regain your position in the line up. Your whip can be a useful prod in this situation too! Once the feet are established then you can encourage the head position. Do not use food too often, but vary it, sometimes calling for attention by waving your whip, snapping your fingers or giving little pats on the nose.

Training can easily go wrong at this stage. Attention spans are short and once concentration is lost, irritation, naughtiness and boredom take over. It is not necessary to practise every day. Every other day is enough, and once the pupil has learnt to walk, trot, turn, halt and pose nicely, a once-a-week refresher course is all that is needed.

Always allow enough time to prepare for shows. As mentioned earlier, at least six weeks is needed to condition a horse (provided that it is not actually in bad condition before starting) and to get the feet level and suitably prepared. Six weeks should also be long enough to train the horse to trot well and stand correctly. Nearer the show, allow six days in which time you might shampoo the mane and tail, trim as necessary, and gradually acquire a deep sheen to the coat with lots of grooming. The preparations on the day before the show could take around six hours. The horse, its tack, your outfit and the transport all need attention.

If you are plaiting your horse, it is best to get up early to do this on the morning of the show. Plaits put in the night before can become very irritating to the horse, especially if they are well done and very tight. Most horses will rub them. They

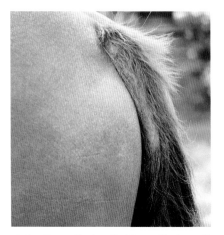

A badly pulled tail. To pull the tail to baldness at the sides, as here, is not only unkind to the horse, it is also extremely ugly. It will be a year at least before this resembles normality, and meanwhile the protection afforded by the tail is lost. It is usually preferable to maintain the tail, plaiting for neatness at shows.

can then become caught on any small projection, with the result that a whole plait could be pulled out by the roots, leaving an ugly gap in the mane. Purebred Arabs, native ponies and palominos are not plaited. If the mane is plaited, then it customary for the tail also to be plaited or pulled. Pulling tails is potentially very dangerous and is resented by many horses. It is probably safer not to pull a youngster's tail. In any case, it is likely to be living out again when showing is over, and will benefit from the protection afforded by a full tail.

Baby oil rubbed over a clean muzzle and around the eyes gives a dark gloss to black skin and enhances the size of the eye. Hooves should be cleaned and oiled inside and out with a dark coloured (but not opaque) oil, to improve, but not disguise, their appearance. You may prefer to use a clear oil on unpigmented hooves. White markings can be brightened by applying chalk block or powder, remembering to whisk off the surplus before going in the ring. Quarter marks, which make a checker board effect on the rump, and other patterns brushed or combed into the coat on the hindquarters, are usually seen only on riding ponies and hacks.

Aim to arrive at the show one hour before your class is due and allow time on the journey for any unforeseen incident such as changing a punctured tyre. Six minutes to go and you should be ready and waiting in the collecting ring, horse immaculate, you smart and wearing your number, which may have been sent to you before show day or which you may have collected from the show secretary on your arrival at the showground.

Having spent so much time on the horse, the handler's turnout also needs attention. For standard British showing, gentlemen wear dark suits and a bowler hat, with pigskin gloves. At less formal shows, a sports or hacking jacket with cavalry twill trousers and a tweed hat or cap may be substituted. Ladies generally wear hacking jacket, shirt and tie, jodhpurs or slacks and jodhpur boots. A hard hat looks smart and is sensible when handling entires. Alternatively, a soft hat may be worn, or perhaps a head scarf. Pigskin gloves are always smart, are hard wearing, and give good protection which is

A nicely turned out team which has been successful in the ring. Note the handler walking in step with her young horse.

essential if the youngster gets excited and pulls. Anything more than very short hair should be held neatly in a net, and longer hair put in a bun.

In some breed classes, variations are seen. Welsh breeds, renowned for their very active trot, are sometimes handled in shirt sleeves and running shoes. In Arab classes, copying the dress used at indoor international shows, handlers sometimes dress all in white, which can look a little bizarre out of doors in variable weather! However, the traditional dress is always correct at outdoor shows for British breeds or types. Foreign breeds will have their own rules and fashions. Taking the trouble to dress according to the dictates of tradition is perceived as correct, safe, and a courtesy to the judge, who is likely to be the smartest person in the ring anyway!

Shows also involve some paperwork. First of all you need to find out when and where shows take place. In March, the two show issues of *Horse and Hound* carry information on the major shows all over Great Britain. Many of the shows carry advertisements which give information additional to just the date and venue, such as affiliations or breeds catered for.

To show at an affiliated show, the horse must be registered with the body to which the show is affiliated, and in many cases, the exhibitor must be a member of that organisation.

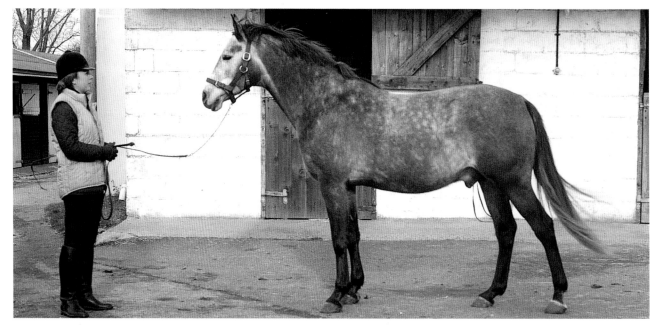

As the horse learns to pose correctly, gradually teach him to accept your standing further away. Three-year-old Anglo-Arab colt.

The judge will be from their approved list, and his or her name is usually given in the schedule. Affiliated shows are usually larger, more professionally run and more prestigious than unaffiliated shows. The standard of horses forward is consequently much higher. The atmosphere of the show will be more formal than that at an unaffiliated show. Some affiliated shows are also qualifiers for major shows later in the year, and competition at these will be especially keen.

Unaffiliated shows make up the majority of small, local shows. Many are run by riding clubs, Pony Club, small agricultural or horticultural societies, or committees based on villages or towns. Often they are raising money for a local charity. Exhibitors will generally be local, so these shows are not usually advertised nationally, but will place notices in the local equestrian press, and may put posters and schedules in saddleries and feed merchants in the area.

Acquiring a schedule is the first stage in entering a show. Send a stamped, self-addressed envelope to the secretary of the show, as printed in *Horse and Hound* or locally. When the schedule arrives, check when the entries close. Some shows, and generally all affiliated shows, will not accept entries after the closing date. Others require a larger fee. Then see what classes your horse is eligible for. Age is often a factor, although sometimes, one, two, and three year olds are judged together. A yearling can sometimes look outclassed when standing next to a three year old, so bear this in mind. Breeds with only a small following may find that there is only one class for all ages, young and adult.

A horse's age is always calculated according to the year of birth, not the actual date. So, if a horse is two in a particular year, it is shown as a two year old for the whole of that year, even before its actual second birthday.

The height of the youngster may be a factor, but it is the height at maturity, not the present height. If the actual height required is not stated in the schedule, refer to Table 2.

Table 2 Maximum heights allowed for youngstock showing (½ inch extra allowed after July)

Height at maturity	Height at one year	Height at two years	Height at three years
12.2 hh	11.3 hh	12.0 hh	12.1 hh
13.2 hh	12.3 hh	13.0 hh	13.1 hh
14.2 hh	13.3 hh	14.0 hh	14.1 hh
15.0 hh	14.1 hh	14.2 hh	14.3 hh
15.3 hh	15.0 hh	15.1 hh	15.2 hh

If your youngster is of a particular breed or registered type, check if the class is for pure or partbreds, and if proof of registration is required, have a photocopy made rather than send off your original, valuable, document. Similarly, if proof of vaccination is required (usually large shows or those on racecourses) check with your vet that it is correct, and make a photocopy of the original document.

If your horse is unregistered, or you are unsure of its type, then the local shows are ideal. Enter for the class which seems appropriate and for which you are eligible. At these smaller shows, the judge is usually very willing to give a brief opinion at the end of the class.

Having chosen your class, fill in the entry form as requested, make sure you have read all the rules, understand them and will abide by them, and then sign the entry form and send it with the correct money to the show's entries secretary. If your exhibitor's number is to be sent to you, it may be necessary to enclose an SAE. If not sent, allow time to collect the number at the show. You will need to wear it, tied around your waist and showing to the back, in the collecting ring and judging ring at the show.

Showing yearlings can be very frustrating. These classes are usually the largest, as everyone is wanting to know whether their young horse is going to be a successful show horse. Attending a limited number of shows at this age can be seen as educational, but in order to win prizes it will almost invariably be necessary to stable the horse for the large majority of the time, and to feed considerably more concentrates than would be needed merely to maintain good health. Such a life style is not to be considered as in the animal's best interests, and can lead to the problems outlined above.

Two year olds can be very rewarding to show, as at this age they seem to be very receptive to new things. Their growth rate has slowed down, and they will naturally look in a condition nearer that required for the ring. Unfortunately, as fewer numbers of two and three year olds are shown than yearlings, these two ages are often put into one class, when a two year old may look at a slight disadvantage against a more mature three year old. By the time the horse is three, maybe you will have had enough of showing and will be more eager instead to continue with its education as a riding horse!

11 GROWING PAINS

Growing up is not always easy and straightforward. Sometimes things go wrong. Occasionally, problems may right themselves, but many will of course need the help of a skilled professional such as your vet or farrier.

If a horse is not sound, it is useless. Any crookedness in the limbs is potential unsoundness. Viewed from the front, the toes of the fore feet should point directly forward, at the bottom of a line that bisects the whole leg perpendicular to the ground. It is quite common for yearlings or two year olds to start turning out one or both toes. As soon as this is spotted, call your farrier who is usually able to sort the problem out by re-balancing the feet. As the toe turns out, more weight comes to bear on the inside of the hoof. Lowering the outside of the wall corrects this imbalance. A good farrier will sort out the problem in a matter of a few weeks.

Yearlings, especially those in light condition or narrow in the chest, may turn both fore feet out slightly and equally. This can be absolutely normal, and will correct itself naturally as the horse fills out and broadens in the chest. The farrier will be able to advise. If the feet are not wearing abnormally he may well feel inclined to leave matters to correct themselves. Abnormal or uneven wear on the feet, however, suggests the problem is more serious and will definitely need attention.

The opposite problem, of the toes turning in, can also occur but is not so common. It is often associated with a horse gaining weight, becoming top-heavy and 'chesty'. It will lead to dishing, too, so needs immediate action again from the farrier who, in this case, will take more horn from the inside

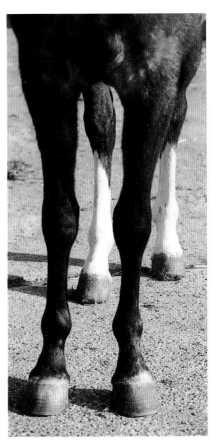

Slight toe-out on a rising three year old. The deviation is mainly in the fetlock joint. This is a potential weakness; the filly is also more likely to brush (knock the fetlock joint with the opposite hoof).

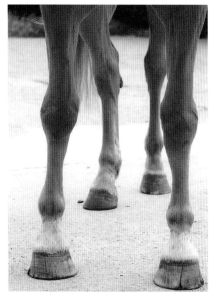

Whilst it is more usual for an immature horse to turn its toes out, sometimes the opposite occurs, as shown here with this young Irish Draught. He is very wide in the chest and even wider between the fetlocks. The toes turn markedly inwards. The crookedness in the legs has put stress on the knees and splints have formed beneath both knees, worryingly close to the joint. Not surprisingly, this horse also dishes. The cracked hooves are an additional source of concern.

Large splint on near fore. Fortunately, it is just clear of the knee (carpus joint) and will not cause serious problems. Turning out to grass is usually best for youngsters with splints.

of the foot. If the horse has become overweight, this, too should be corrected. If the feet and weight are not normalised, the horse will have an increased susceptibility to splints on the inside of the fore legs below the knee, due to the increased stress on the misaligned limb.

Splints are very common. They appear as hard, bony swellings, usually (but not always) on the fore legs between the knee and mid-cannon, on the inside of the leg. So-called false splints are due to a knock — perhaps the youngster kicking itself, a kick from a field companion or even a careless tap from a hard-backed grooming brush. Such lumps, although unsightly, rarely cause trouble and in time should go completely. True splints are more to do with a defect in the horse than a mere accident. They are specifically a bony lump forming between the splint bone and the cannon bone. In young horses, the splint bone is separated from the cannon bone by a ligament. Part of the ageing process involves the fusing of these two bones, but until they are fused, uneven pressure at the knee (carpal) joint may cause the splint bone to shift slightly, tearing the ligament and the periosteum to which it is attached. A bony outgrowth — a splint — results. Small, weak knees are predisposing, but the main causes are conformational deviations. Offset cannons frequently develop splints. The cannon bone is offset to the outside of the knee joint. A splint commonly forms just below the knee, very conspicuous when it first forms. Careful examination will reveal that it remains forever, albeit smaller, because the bony outgrowth is gradually, but not completely, resorbed over time. Crooked legs, where the toe is noticeably turned in or out, are also more prone to splints, but not usually as high as those resulting from offset cannons. Large, high splints are called knee splints and are considered serious due to the possible interference in the function of the knee joint.

False splints may lose you a place or two in the show ring; true splints could see you move a long way down the line-up. The vet will be able to diagnose the type of splint and its likely consequences.

Just as splints may or may not be a cause for concern, so too are curbs. A curb is a lump on the back of the lower part of the hock about a hand's-breadth below the point of hock. A true curb is the result of damage to the ligament which goes round the joint at this point. It is considered serious as it suggests that the hock, a vitally important joint, is not sufficiently strong to withstand the rigours of work. A false curb is due to the bone in that area being more prominently developed, and is on occasions seen in yearlings and two year olds. By the time they are mature, they seem to have 'grown into' the false curb, which never causes them any bother. Again, it is a question of diagnosis: the vet's job!

An imbalanced diet can be implicated in many leg development problems, so if you are at all concerned, it is wise to consult your vet or an independent equine nutritionist. The higher the level of 'hard' feed as opposed to hay and grass, the greater the risk of a feeding imbalance and hence a developmental problem. Aim to keep the diet as simple as possible with as little grain as possible. Young horses should never be allowed to become overweight — their bones are just not hard enough or strong enough to cope with the extra load.

Hernia is a congenital problem seen occasionally. Although the problem is present at birth (a gap in the abdominal muscle near the umbilicus through which a loop of gut protrudes, ballooning the skin to form a soft swelling from the size of a small egg up to the size of a grapefruit), it does not always show until the foal is eating more bulky food at around the age of three months. Small hernias often go on their own, usually by the time the horse is around eighteen months, but until they go, your chances of showing success are reduced and there is always the possibility that the hernia may strangulate — that is, the muscle layer closes in, trapping the loop of gut. This will cause a severe colic and death if not dealt with. Gently manipulating the hernia back in each day reduces this risk. If the hernia is not going to go on its own, it will need operating on. Your vet will advise you on this, but as the youngster will need to be kept in for a few weeks while it is recovering from what is major surgery, it seems unfair to have it done in the summer when your horse should be out enjoying the grass. It seems more reasonable to have such surgery done in the autumn or winter, when it would be

This thoroughbred yearling has slightly 'curby' hocks — note the slight prominence on the lower back part of the hock. This could disappear as the youngster grows. The large, 'appley' fetlock joints, looking disproportionate to the slender pasterns, may be a warning of a future weakness.

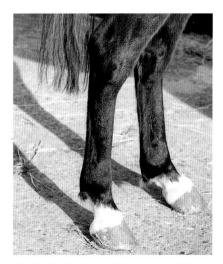

Weak hocks on a three year old. The joint lacks depth (tied in below the hock); it is slightly over-angulated (sickle hocked) and is slightly capped on the point of hock. Hard, fast work could injure such hocks.

Capped hock − not actually an unsoundness but more likely on small joints, as here.

The odd appearance of Jamborino's knee is due to the open growth plate (epiphysis) at the end of his forearm (radius). This is typical in yearlings.

more likely to be stabled for at least part of the day anyway. Discuss it with your vet, who, hopefully, will arrange for the operation to be done at a veterinary school where your horse will have an experienced surgeon, excellent facilities, the best care and you will also have the satisfaction of knowing that his little problem has helped to instruct the next generation of veterinary surgeons!

In many other species, the tendency to have a hernia is inherited. This has not been proved beyond doubt in horses, but it does seem to run in families, so it may be sensible not to breed from a horse which has had a hernia repaired.

As the bones and teeth develop, changes of shape occur too. The lower leg stops growing early on, but the forearm (radius) of the yearling grows at its distal end, just above the knee. While it is growing, the knee may look knobbly and a distinct horizontal dent can be seen across the knee. This is all absolutely normal, but a youngster with 'open' knees, as they are termed, does not want to suffer undue concussion, so it may be wise to avoid shows at this stage. Young thoroughbreds going into training often have their knees X-rayed to ensure that the growing points (epiphyses) are fully developed and have closed.

Damage or developmental problems at the epiphyses can give rise to a disease called epiphysitis. It usually affects older foals and yearlings, and is most commonly seen in the knees. It can be caused by concussion on hard ground, over feeding or an imbalanced diet lacking available calcium. Sufferers are often on diets with high levels of grain, which could also be leading to unnaturally fast growth rates. The veterinary surgeon will probably suggest that the diet is reduced nutritionally but increased in its levels of fibre. A lame youngster will need to be rested in the stable, but once free of pain it should be returned to a normal life style, with plenty of exercise and a balanced diet, possibly with a calcium supplement. Epiphysitis is very much more unusual in young horses fed on forage-based rather than grain-based diets.

Hind legs often grow ahead of fore legs so growing horses go through stages of being 'up behind' until the forehand catches up. Again this is quite normal, but obviously balance

Fore limb

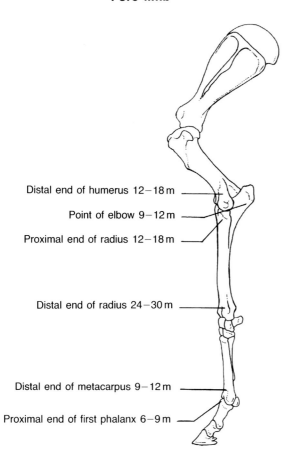

Distal end of humerus 12−18 m

Point of elbow 9−12 m

Proximal end of radius 12−18 m

Distal end of radius 24−30 m

Distal end of metacarpus 9−12 m

Proximal end of first phalanx 6−9 m

Hind limb

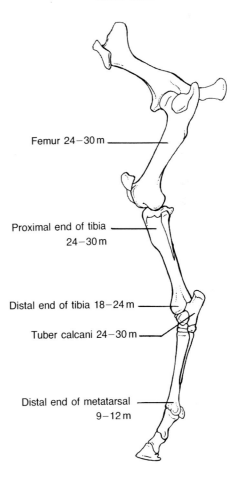

Femur 24−30 m

Proximal end of tibia
24−30 m

Distal end of tibia 18−24 m

Tuber calcani 24−30 m

Distal end of metatarsal
9−12 m

Times of epiphyseal closure. The
spinal column continues to grow
until around five years of age.

is altered. The shoulder will appear more upright and the horse will have a shorter stride and go on his forehand.

Clicking can sometimes be heard in the joints of the hind leg. It is usually the stifle joint making the noise. Often, it is just a temporary problem and will disappear as the horse levels up. However, there are some serious developmental problems which can occur in the stifle or other hind leg joints, so if there is any suggestion that the clicking is associated with pain or discomfort, or the horse's action is affected in any way, a check up from the vet could be a wise precaution. Thoroughbreds and their crosses are occasionally prone to a joint disorder, osteochondrosis, which is serious and for which you will need urgent veterinary advice.

Osteochondrosis is a degenerative disease of the cartilage in the joints. It is seen most often in the hind legs, where the joints usually affected are the hock and the stifle. It causes lameness and the affected joint may be swollen and tender.

It seems that horses growing rapidly are most at risk, and those with an upright conformation of the hind leg, known as 'post leg'. Possibly this lack of the normal amount of angulation in the leg increases the levels of concussion in the joints. If the osteochondrosis develops further, the cartilage may even start to disintegrate, a condition termed osteochondrosis disecans. Any degree of this condition is likely to have a long-term effect on the joint and will adversely affect the horse's capacity for work, so the veterinary surgeon is needed not only to diagnose and treat the disease (if possible) but also to offer an opinion on the prognosis for the future.

The limbs will have completed most of their growth by the time the horse is 2½ years old, but the body will deepen and develop for another year or so. The bones of the back do not finally stop growing and harden until the horse is five years old.

Navicular disease was thought to be a problem generally of older horses, but is now, with advances in diagnostic techniques, seen to have its early impact in young horses even before they start work. This disorder affects the navicular bone, a small sesamoid bone protecting the deep flexor tendon where it passes behind the lowest joint of the horse's leg, the coffin joint. This is the junction of the short pastern (os coronae) with the coffin or pedal bone, the os pedis. Bruising and blood clots in the bone eventually lead to its surface becoming roughened, pitted and, eventually, ulceration can erode a hole right through it.

Horses with small, shallow feet are more prone to it, or horses with normal feet which have been injudiciously trimmed and the heels lowered too much. Sudden, jarring trotting following a period of immobility is thought to be a trigger. When stationary, the blood circulating in the feet is about one tenth of that circulating following gentle exercise. A show horse, standing in line, then expected to show at extended trot, is believed to be at an increased risk of developing navicular disease. Shallow or over trimmed feet bring the navicular bone closer to the ground and so it is more likely to be bruised. Hard ground and an overweight horse add to the problem. Insufficient blood circulating in the foot reduces the system's ability to repair damage, and so the early stages of the disease could ensue.

Signs of navicular disease include a shortened stride, lameness on turns, stumbling and resting one (or each in turn) fore foot by 'pointing' it. The horse holds the foot up to 12 inches (30 cm) or so in front of the other fore foot, with little weight on it and the pastern aligned with the cannon bone. This has the effect of taking weight off the deep flexor tendon, which otherwise bears some of the horse's weight. In a susceptible horse, which may have low heels, the navicular bone is compressed between the deep flexor tendon and the coffin joint. It may be noticed that the horse's toes are wearing, as it is trying to keep its weight forward, off the painful navicular bone, which is situated relatively near the heels. In action, the horse may be attempting to place the foot toe first on the ground, instead of flat at slow speeds, and heel first when extending.

A young horse showing early signs of navicular disease should be allowed to grow a little more foot, then be trimmed by a knowledgeable farrier who will leave the heels a little deeper, and the toes a little shorter, to restore a more comfortable balance in the foot, and a rounder shape to the hoof. An overweight horse should have all hard feed cut out, to reduce this problem. Time at grass should be increased to twenty-four hours a day if possible. Even 'mooching' about in a little paddock will give a level of blood circulation in the foot above that likely when the horse is confined to the stable.

With a condition such as this, which could have serious consequences if not corrected promptly (permanent unsoundness), the veterinary surgeon's advice should, of course, be sought. He may administer pain relief and drugs to improve the circulation of blood in the tiny capillaries of the foot.

Herbalists recommend garlic in the diet, which is believed also to improve periferal circulation, by slightly decreasing the blood's viscosity.

Yearlings have fine, neat heads. Their jaws hold their small-rooted milk teeth. But from the age of two, this all changes. The massive, permanent molars develop and fill the jaws almost to bursting point. The lower jaw looks heavy, with an undulating outline. Each bump represents the thinnest layer of jawbone over an enormous molar root. Sometimes, bumps appear on the front of the face, just below the eyes, when space in a small head is just not enough for the huge teeth. It

Trincamalee, three-year-old Arab filly, shows clearly the double bump in the lower jaw, caused by the roots of the huge molars.

is quite clear that tight nosebands and chain lead reins under the jaw will cause unnecessary discomfort – in fact, some youngsters are happier being shown with a bit rather than a tight chain over their painful developing molars. As the years pass, the teeth are worn at the crown from eating and gradually the teeth move up through the jaw, the jaw-bone retreating behind them. Between five and seven years of age, 'tooth bumps' will finally go – later, in old age, it will be noticed that the jaws are curving inwards, nosebands all seem too large – the head has 'dried out' (odd term!) and the next stage will be for the teeth to wear out and be lost altogether.

If your youngster is a filly, she is destined to come into oestrus every three weeks throughout the breeding season. Although, as with colts, stock from her generally cannot be registered unless she was over twenty-four months when covered, this is not to say that she cannot conceive below this age. In the spring following the year of her birth, as a yearling, a filly is likely to have her first serious heat. Many filly foals show some sign of oestrus, but this first proper one may alter her behaviour considerably. She will be uncomfortable and confused. The sudden attention paid her by her field companions may upset her. Her hormones and her instincts are giving conflicting messages. Although mares are in season for five or six days generally, fillies are more irregular both in the timing and frequency of their heats. Although it is of course absolutely normal, it may be better to avoid new things when a filly is in season and it would certainly be unwise to show her in mixed classes with colts when she is 'horsing'. As she gets older, her seasons may have a less noticeable effect on her temperament and she will have to learn to carry on as usual.

There are so many things which can go wrong with a young horse when it is growing up. Some of the problems may be unavoidable accidents, some may be due to an unwise policy of the breeder, and some will be down to misman-agement. It is natural to want to do the best for your young horse but, in striving for perfection, it is important to remember that for 55 million years nature has managed quite well without the benefit of human interference. The single

Her raised tail and her approaches to Banjo show that Blue is in season in the summer of her yearling year.

Three yearlings enjoying a canter with a four-year-old companion.

most important thing for a growing horse is space. With room to wander at will, the horse will acquire muscular tone and fitness, and the developmental processes are more likely to continue normally. There is no substitute for good grazing, which is superior in every way to any artificial feed given to stabled horses. Company will ensure that the youngster plays and socialises.

Horses at grass in groups will play, especially colts, and will, inevitably, get the occasional mark on them. This is a small price to pay for the benefits of a natural lifestyle.

Growing youngsters at the greatest risk of developmental problems and injuries are those which are stabled most of the time, fed above their nutritional requirements, and turned out for only short periods, possibly on their own. Long hours of confinement do not encourage strong bones, ligaments, tendons or muscles, but the high levels of feeding give the horse surplus energy. When it is let out it goes mad, its plump, overweight body straining unfit muscles and sinews. On its own, it will try to join any other horse it can see or hear, and in company, its play will be boisterous and rough. This all leads to injury, none of which would occur in a horse at liberty for the majority of its time.

The occasional minor injury will soon heal; developmental problems leave a legacy of reduced performance ability, if not outright unsoundness.

Colts reared in mixed age groups with geldings are rarely any trouble. They have plenty of opportunity to exercise and play. Justinus, yearling colt, follows two yearling and two four-year-old geldings.

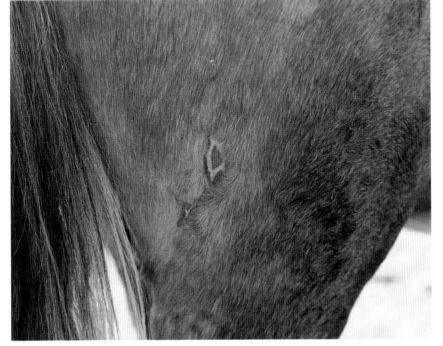

A healing wound on the thigh of a yearling.

12 FEEDING

Of the 55 million years during which equines have been evolving, breeding and managing perfectly well without human intervention, for the last 30 million or so, the equid family have been grazers. As their size increased over the millennia, more food was needed to maintain their ever bulkier bodies. Having committed themselves to grass, which is not only tough but not terribly nutritious, two other things had to develop as well: massive teeth that would not wear out too soon ahead of the rest of the horse, and an insatiable urge to eat almost non-stop. As grazers, the species has managed to survive on the open plains and steppes that are a horse's natural home. We, however, want our horses not only to survive as a species, which is nature's aim, but to thrive as individuals. The occasional late-born foal failing to make it through the winter may be one of the risks of the natural order, but if such losses are not going to happen to our horses, a little human intervention will be necessary. On close inspection, it is possible to see how totally and completely most modern horses have been removed from their ancestral home and their basic, natural, way of life.

Horses are herd animals. They feel safe and secure with others of their species around them. Being almost defenceless, several eyes and ears are better at picking up potential danger than the one set of a solitary individual. When it is quiet, large herds split up into small groups, often based on families. When danger threatens, the groups may gather and if the threat seems real, they will all flee en masse. A young horse kept in an individual stable is bound to feel nervous and

Good grazing is always a horse keeper's best feeding asset. At the end of October, yearling Arab, Jenerous, is keeping well on good grazing alone.

(*Opposite*) Two-and-a-half-year-old Chieftain with a week's supply of food. He is currently around 15.2 hands high, weighs about 400 kg (900 lb) and eats 10 kg of food a day (22 lb).

101

Two-year-old fillies turned out in mid November with mares and their foals aged six months or more. Groups of mixed ages are natural and usually very stable. This grazing is currently providing enough fibre. One feed a day, in the field, meets the additional needs due to colder weather and lower feed value of the grass. Soon additional hay will also be needed.

jumpy — it has no one else helping to look out for danger, and nowhere to run to if danger does appear. It can see some space over the stable door, but, frustratingly, cannot get out. This can result in the horse becoming a weaver, for instance. Weaving is a repetitive swaying or pacing back and forth, usually in front of the door. Before long the habit becomes ingrained as a committed behavioural pattern, and is likely to remain with the horse for life, even if later on its circumstances improve. The anxiety of confinement is compounded when concentrated food is given. The horse's nutritional requirements are quite easily met with suitable cubes or mixes, but they are consumed quickly. It will look well, but that primeval urge to eat for around fourteen to sixteen hours out of every twenty-four is not met. Nature is telling the horse to eat for all it is worth in order to get enough nourishment from the natural but low-grade food. But in a few hours good hay and delicious hard feed, quite sufficient food value, are gone. So the horse will look for something else, and may turn to straw bedding. Changing to wood chips may prevent bed eating but the urge to consume a large bulk of food can remain unsatisfied. Consequently, the horse may resort to chewing any available woodwork in the stable and could also become nippy with his handlers. The cause of these problems is clearly lack of bulky food and is not best served by finding ways to prevent bed-eating or wood-chewing.

On a high-grade diet, the horse's urge to eat continues after its nutritional requirements have been met, but, similarly, under conditions of starvation on very short, poor pasture, the horse will not significantly extend its eating time in order to make up for the shortfall.

A growing horse has greater nutritional needs than a mature horse. It needs more calcium to produce bones and teeth. It needs more protein to build muscle. It needs more digestible carbohydrate for energetic playing and spooking. In the wild, it would get milk from the dam until it was getting on for a year old, by which time the spring grass, full of nourishment, is growing. Nature will be telling it to make the most of it and even to get fat, if possible, because there may not be much to eat come next winter. This is where we can do better than nature − instead of storing a surplus as fat, we can make hay so we can provide the goodness of early summer grass all year.

Once a horse has acquired a taste for wood, it will find any untreated timber attractive, especially softwoods.

Andalusian youngsters, southwest Spain. Not all climates result in good grass; these youngsters will need most of their feed brought to them, in this case lucerne hay and barley meal with supplements.

Malnutrition, as in this youngster rescued by the Ada Cole Memorial Stables, can result in limb defects. Both toes turn out. The crookedness is in the whole leg, especially the off fore.

Most domesticated horses have to be confined to a greater or lesser extent. Even large stud farms are only a fraction of the size of an original wild horse's steppes. So, although domesticated horses can fare better food-wise, they do suffer from being forced to graze the same small area all year. Worms are a major problem. All horses have them; they never become immune to worms, especially red worms (strongyles) which do extensive damage to guts, blood vessels and even major organs of the body, as the larvae migrate through the horse's body before returning to the gut to complete their development, mature and mate, and for the females to lay millions of eggs to be passed out in the droppings. Even so-called 'wild' ponies, which are actually feral, being distant descendants of previously domesticated ponies, have a worm problem, as encroaching civilisation has made their native heaths and moorlands smaller and more crowded.

When formulating a diet for a young horse, it is important to meet the nutritional requirements, remove the opposition (in the form of worms), but not to forget the need for fibre. Not only do horses have a psychological urge to eat plenty of bulk, but the digestive system has evolved to function best on a bulky, fibrous diet.

Meadow hay is finer, softer, composed of more species and more easily digested than 'hard' hay. Quality is also more variable. This is a good sample, still showing some green colour fifteen months after it was made.

Good quality forage (hay, grass and so on) must be the basis of feeding. Concentrates (cubes, mixes, straights such as oats or barley) should be fed to make up any nutritional shortfall. It is possible on good, well-managed pasture in the summer that your young horse will not need any supplementary feeding. Certainly native ponies should not need extra feeding when on good grass. If they are failing to thrive, it is reasonable to suppose that there is some other problem, such as worms, a tooth problem or possibly even something more sinister such as ragwort poisoning.

Not only does grass provide essential roughage, but it also contains vitamins and minerals. Spring grass also provides good levels of protein and soluble carbohydrate. You may notice the effect of the grass coming through in the spring when a growing horse that seems to have ceased to grow over the winter will suddenly have an upward surge of growth in the spring and early summer. Nature's way of making the most of the situation!

Spring grass on good, well-managed land, which may also have been artificially fertilised, may in fact be so rich in sugars and low in fibre as to cause scouring (diarrhoea) and possibly even laminitis, too. On such rich grass it may be necessary to provide supplementary fibre in the form of old, but clean, hay, or even a good sample of straw.

When feeding concentrates, which will probably be necessary for all young stock in the winter, it is important to maintain the correct balance of minerals as well as providing sufficient vitamins. The balance of amino acids in the protein also needs attention. Amino acids are like building blocks from which different proteins are constructed. Different amino acids are present in proteins from different sources. If you are thinking that this all sounds as if it could get complicated, you are right! Fortunately, there are now some very good nuts and mixes available, carefully formulated to meet the requirements of all stock. All you have to do is make sure you get the correct one for your young horse – usually a stud mix will be the one. Unless you are preparing fast-growing thoroughbred yearlings for the autumn sales, so-called yearling cubes are best avoided, as under other circumstances they can be too

A mixed sward of grasses and herbs in an old meadow – superb grazing for all stock. Always check for poisonous plants such as ragwort which should be hand-pulled, ensuring all the root is removed, and burnt.

(*Right*) Cutting lucerne on the Dengie Peninsular in Essex. (*Above*) The wilted lucerne is taken to the factory for rapid drying before distribution as pellets or coarse chop.

high-powered, providing nutrients for a rapid development not normally required, or even beneficial, in other breeds.

In countries where lucerne (alfalfa) grows well, it has been found that horses thrive and develop well on it. Cooler places, like Britain, have only a few areas where it will grow at all, but now production has been increased and dried lucerne is available in different forms. It is an excellent feed for all young horses, containing all the nutritional requirements of youngstock except carbohydrate. This author has had considerable experience with dried lucerne products and has successfully fed mares, foals and yearlings with no other feed than hay or grass. If a little more condition is required or, for instance, it is very cold or wet, additional carbohydrate may be needed. A mix or cube can be used, or if straights are preferred, oats or barley.

Research has shown that the protein in, for instance, lucerne, can be relatively easily converted to carbohydrate during digestion. Amino acids are, in effect, a carbohydrate with a nitrogen containing portion tacked on the end. The removal of the nitrogenous portion is quite easily achieved and the remaining carbohydrate can be used as energy for activity and keeping warm or can be converted to fat for storage.

Barley has a higher feed value than oats, but oats have some as yet unidentified ingredient which makes many horses, and especially ponies, very lively. The choice of grain is a fairly individual matter, but it must be remembered that all grains (and especially barley and maize) are low in fibre and contain phytins which are substances which rob the diet of calcium. Grains are already deficient in calcium; diets too dependent on grains can lead to bone development disorders. Further, grains are short of an amino acid, lysine. Luckily, there is one product that can sort all this out in one! Dried sugar beet pulp has good levels of fibre, calcium and lysine. It is an ideal balancer when cereals are used in the diet. It is also very much enjoyed by horses and must have quite a strong flavour, for if medicines, such as worm doses, are first mixed with sugar beet and then into the ration, most horses will eat them without hesitation.

Sugar beet comes in dried form, as loose shreds, pellets or cubes. It *must not* be used for horses until it has been thoroughly soaked in water. It will swell up to three (shreds) or five (cubes) times its original bulk following soaking. Weight for weight, it should be soaked in five times its weight of water, so one kilogram of sugar beet should be soaked in five litres of water. In cold water, this can take up to twenty-four

Fibrous food is vital for horses. Here are some examples, clockwise from bottom left:
(1) Carrots
(2) Chaff (or, more correctly, 'chop')
(3) Molassed sugar beet pellets.
(4) Unmolassed sugar beet pellets.
(5) Alfa A (chopped, dried lucerne).
(6) Alfalfa (dried, pelleted lucerne).

Jenerous obviously enjoying his new grazing.

hours. It is quicker in hot water, but it must not be fed to horses until the soaking and swelling process is complete. Once wet, the sugar in the beet can ferment, especially in warm weather. Alcohol is produced first, then acetic acid (vinegar). In warm weather, no more than one day's supply should be soaked at a time. In winter, no more than two day's supply.

If dried lucerne and cereal grain are fed in equal amounts by weight, and a volume of soaked sugar beet added, equal to the volume of the grain, a balanced diet should result, needing only ad lib hay or grass to complete it. A mineralised salt lick should be available at all times. However, different horses have different nutritional requirements. It is vital to react promptly to any problem which could be diet related. In a growing horse, this is not just a matter of whether it is fat or thin, but also whether the limbs are developing normally and straight, that the youngster has sufficient energy for playing, that the coat and hooves are in good condition and that it does not have an appetite which is in any way depraved. Excessive eating of droppings, soil, bark from trees or licking walls, for instance, can all suggest an imbalance somewhere. If there is any problem, real or imagined, it is of course sensible to consult your vet or a qualified equine nutritionist.

Chieftain's weekly supply of food consists of hay, carrots, and (from left to right) sugar beet, alfalfa pellets (in bag), Spillers horse and pony cubes, and Dengie Hi Fi.

Fit and healthy on good summer pasture: three yearlings and two four year olds.

It is normal for a foal to eat droppings occasionally, in order for it to acquire its gut bacteria. Older horses may sometimes eat droppings to re-establish the gut flora after stress or antibiotic therapy has disrupted it, but in other than these instances, dung eating is likely to indicate a problem, such as insufficient fibre in the diet.

Feeding is both an art and a science, which has been developed and refined over the years. Much of what was written one hundred years ago can still hold good today, but some more recent research has shown that some old-fashioned methods of feeding may have caused problems. Old literature refers constantly to the use of bran for all classes of stock. Modern milling methods now remove more of the flour and hence feed value from the bran, but more than that, it has been shown that bran can cause serious problems with calcium uptake. It is itself low in calcium, and also high in phytins. Its low feed value, high cost and potential risk to bone development have resulted in few authorities now recommending its use. Other products achieve some of its benefits in a far more satisfactory way. Bulk can be added to the diet by using chop (chaff) which is sold in a molassed form and made from chopped hay or straw. Even better is chopped, dried lucerne (alfalfa). Soaked sugar beet can also be used in this way. Chop and soaked sugar beet mixed together with a little boiling water makes a good substitute for bran mash and is nutritionally better. It is also a 'safe' feed for ponies prone to laminitis.

This Shetland has laminitis, which can be seen by her stance – leaning back on the heels of her fore feet, in an attempt to relieve the pain at the front of the feet.

Frequently, the feeding of milk pellets or powder is recommended for young horses. However, after its first winter it is not natural for a horse to consume milk, a feed designed exclusively for infant mammals. A naturally weaned foal will have no need for supplementary milk, nor will a foal sensibly weaned when sufficiently old, that is, over seven and a half months. Milk supplements are made from cow's milk, which is ideal only for calves anyway. There are also ethical objections to feeding animals unnecessarily on food produced for people when there are so many starving children in the world. Milk sugar (lactose) is digested by lactase, an enzyme which is produced most copiously in foals. Its production declines rapidly after the natural weaning age, and it is not produced at all in horses over three years of age. Feeding milk in the absence of lactase can lead to digestive or even metabolic disorders.

The amount of concentrated (hard) feed a youngster needs depends on its initial condition, how fast it is growing, its general health, the weather or ambient temperature and how fat you require it to be. More concentrates will be needed if it is under stress, playing hard with boisterous friends or is being bullied by belligerent older horses. As different factors apply at different times, it is necessary to look critically at your youngster on at least a weekly basis, and to make adjustments to the diet before the need to do so becomes obvious. As they say, 'the eye of the master keepeth the horse fat'.

In winter it is likely that the grass is not growing and so your young horse is not getting anything fresh or succulent to eat. In dull, gloomy weather, and with short days, the nutritional value of any grass growth is inevitably going to be low. Feed-grade carrots can often provide a much relished treat in the winter. Feed merchants may provide them or perhaps a greengrocer will be glad to let you have damaged or misshapen carrots cheaply — especially late on a Saturday afternoon! Carrots are traditionally fed sliced lengthwise into 'fingers', but if they are left whole (so long as they are sound) they will keep the horse amused for longer. It will thoroughly enjoy gnawing on them. Carrots should never be cut cross-wise, nor other vegetables cut into similar chunks. A greedy horse could swallow one of these chunks, which might get stuck in the throat, choking the horse. A choke is rarely fatal but is very distressing to both the horse and the owner. The vet should be called immediately. Swedes, turnips, mangles and other large roots can also be fed in this way. Never feed rotten vegetables, and knock off any soil remaining on roots before feeding. If hay is in short supply, it is possible to feed more than the usual 1−2 lb (0.5−1.0 kg) of roots a day − even 7−12 lb (3−5 kg) can be fed daily, provided that the increase is gradual (all changes of diet should be phased over a week to allow the digestive system to adapt to the new routine). It is important to make sure that all the food is cleared up each day so it does not go rotten. If there are any left-overs it would suggest that you have over-fed that item!

Carrots are a most valuable winter feed having useful amounts of carotene, the precursor of vitamin A, which is one of the sunshine vitamins. Summer grazing has plentiful amounts of this important vitamin, but it can be seriously lacking in winter diets.

Autumn grazing, provided it has been well cared for, can be sufficiently nutritious to keep young horses. These two (a three year old and a yearling) look fat and well in a field which has had three months' rest and recuperation after a hay crop before being used again.

A surplus of grass can be mown for hay in late June or July. Haymaking takes around six days in good weather and requires daily turning, or 'tedding'. Here, a Lely Acrobat turns recently mown hay for the first time, fluffing up the drying grass to speed the curing process. Suitably adjusted, the same machine rows up the hay into windrows ready for baling.

New Holland baler produces bales which are collected in a 'flat 8' bale collector...

...and are picked up by the 'flat 8' grabber...

...for loading on to the trailer. Neat stacking and the use of wagon ropes over the load ensure that all the bales survive the short journey home to the barn.

Not all horses are blessed with the best coat. Even on good feeding, some fail to have a really good shine. Adding vegetable oil to the feed can help. A daily dose of 1–2 tbsp (15–30 ml) of sunflower oil can give a shiny coat and also speed up the coat change when the horse moults in the spring. The old-fashioned way was to cook linseed: the seeds need soaking overnight, simmering for about four hours and boiling for ten minutes. This removes the cyanide poisoning which is naturally occurring in linseed. It is far easier to feed sunflower oil! Don't use reject frying oil as it could be rancid and will absorb Vitamin E from the horse, causing a deficiency. Cod liver oil is often recommended and can be very useful if the horse is a bit run down, especially in the winter. It is high in the 'sunshine' vitamins, of which D is the main one, the other being Vitamin A. Vitamins E and K are the other oil-soluble vitamins. Vitamin D is manufactured by the horse in the presence of sunlight and is present in hay that enjoyed good sunny weather when it was made. In the winter, if there is a very prolonged spell of dark and gloomy weather, and the hay is perhaps not so good, then your yearling might benefit from cod liver oil. Use a grade of oil specified for horses and use no more than the recommended amounts. If he gets warm following exercise, you might notice a slight fishy smell.

Unless acting on veterinary advice, it is not wise to start adding supplements to the diet, especially ones favouring a particular mineral. An excess of one thing can cause a deficiency of something else. Calcium and phosphorus work in balance in this way. It is better to add a balanced supplement.

Poor hooves can often benefit from the addition of seaweed to the feed. Again, it is important to feed the correct, recommended amount, even with a natural product like this. Too much can upset the balance of iodine in the horse and lead to thyroid problems.

Keep an eye on your youngster, and be ready for problems but don't anticipate them. Good management will significantly reduce the likelihood of problems occurring.

The daily amount of feed taken by an individual horse is very variable, but generally they will eat around 2½ per cent of their own body weight in dry food. Some of this will be

Make hay while the sun shines, and ask your friends and relations to help get it safely home!

forage (hay, grass etc.) and the balance hard feed. Until work starts, the growing horse will need a decreasing proportion of hard feed and an increasing proportion of fibrous food. This is because the rate of growth, creating the requirement for 'hard' feed, gradually reduces. At the same time, the requirement for protein gradually declines from 14 per cent of the diet in the first winter, to around 8–10 per cent in maturity. As the horse's body grows, so to do the organs within it, and in particular the caecum. The horse's capacity, and need, for fibre increases, too.

In practice, it usually works out that the young horse eats the same weight of hard feed as it will when mature and in light to moderate work, only dropping below this when three years old, and before work starts. The amount of hay eaten increases considerably. The hard feed ration of the youngster will contain a higher level of protein than will be needed once adulthood has been reached. But good summer grazing, remember, is likely to meet these nutritional requirements without supplementation. This guide is most appropriate to winter feeding.

Table 3 is a guide, the example given being a horse to mature at 1000 lb (450 kg) such as an Arab, Thoroughbred hack or small riding horse. For other breeds or types, the proportions are similar although of course the weights will vary. New research from Australia suggest that current recommended protein levels, as shown here, may be over generous.

Table 3 Feeding youngstock

	% protein	Ratio hay: hard feed	% of adult weight	Approx. amount/day eaten (1000 lb adult weight)
Weaned foal	14	1:1	45%	11 lb
Yearling	12–13	2:1	55%	14 lb
2 yr old	11–12	3:1	80%	20 lb
3 yr old	10–11	4:1	90%	22 lb

13 TRAVELLING

Travelling can be traumatic and even dangerous, but both these factors can be reduced to a minimum if a conscious effort is made to reduce risks.

It is very important that the vehicle is powerful enough and has sufficiently low gearing to enable it not only to travel on the flat, but also to pull away smoothly from stationary on a hill.

If a trailer is used, its laden weight should not exceed that of the towing vehicle, or the maximum weight suggested for towing in the manufacturer's handbook. A manual gearbox is preferable to an automatic. If a horsebox is a conversion, or an adaptation to a light goods vehicle or a van, consult the handbook for maximum laden weights. Remember that the gross vehicle weight must include the weight not only of the horses, but their tack, feed, and handlers, too. Alterations to the suspension, strengthening it for its live cargo, may also add to the gross weight. Make good use of your nearest public weighbridge if you are in any doubt.

Most horses travel better if they are partitioned in quite closely. They are less likely to be thrown off balance as they can lean on the partitions to balance going round corners. It is also easier for the driver to drive safely, especially with a trailer, because a horse moving around will considerably alter the balance of a vehicle.

The partitions should be solid and strong, going all the way to the floor. Small gaps can trap hooves and larger gaps can cause a serious injury if a horse goes down (falls). There is also the risk of tread injuries from the horse travelling in the

115

adjacent compartment. Gates therefore are most unsuitable as partitions for any horses.

The floor should be strong and non-slip. Wooden floors are the usual choice being shock-absorbent, much quieter than steel and more rigid than aluminium. However, they need careful maintenance to prevent rotting, and the muck should be removed promptly after each journey. The junction of the floor with the wall is also prone to rotting. There are several types of non-slip flooring available which may be laid over the original wooden flooring of horseboxes and trailers. Rubber has the added benefit of being relatively quiet underfoot and absorbing more of the bumps and vibrations of travelling. But whatever the flooring, most horses, and especially young ones, will travel much better if the floor is covered with their familiar bedding material, even taking it from the horse's own stable so that its smell is familiar, too. Straw should be well shaken and the box left open for ten minutes or so to allow any dust to disperse. The confined atmosphere of many horse-boxes will itself increase the risk of coughing without dust from straw adding to the problem. Unless the box is very well ventilated, humidity and dust levels can rise dramatically during a journey, compromising the horse's health.

The walls need to be strong enough to withstand kicking. Cladding with rubber matting or impact-absorbing boards protects not only the vehicle, but also the horse's legs from injury.

It is surprising how much better some horses travel if they can see out. Perhaps being able to see through a window helps them to balance. Windows should be made of toughened, laminated glass and suitably protected with bars, especially if within the horse's reach. Sliding windows help in providing ventilation, which, as already mentioned, is very important when travelling. Lorries can be fitted with translucent tops, which increase the light in the box. In sunny weather this can result in overheating, so extra ventilation is needed. The air needs to be let out as well as in if the atmosphere is to keep fresh, ideally without causing a chill draught along the horse's back. Extractor fans in the roof are suitable to provide this additional ventilation.

It is very common for horses to sweat to varying degrees, especially at the start of a journey or until they have settled down. Do not be over-enthusiastic with the rugs unless you are certain the horse needs them. Overheated, uncomfortable and sweating, it is more likely to become agitated and start kicking. Rugs should be used only if the horse is well accustomed to them. They should fit well and be firmly, comfortably secured with fitted cross-surcingles or a roller. It is important that they do not slip on the journey, because this can upset the horse and it is putting the handler at risk when attempts are made to remedy the situation in the close confines of a trailer or horse box.

Make sure there is no pressure on the spine. Even padded rollers can cause some pressure, and may well need extra padding, such as a folded piece of blanket. Foam rubber or plastic is not recommended as it compresses, leaving the roller loose and liable to slip. It is also very hot and may result in sweating or further discomfort.

Hay often helps the horse to settle on the journey, but again, thought needs to be given to the potential problem of dust. If good hay is well-shaken before being put into nets, the risk is reduced. Suspect or dusty hay should not be used. Thorough soaking can be followed by careful draining, but haylage in one of its many commercial forms is the best choice for journeys. Haylage is made by compressing wilted grass into sealed, air-tight, plastic bags. A gentle fermentation process preserves the product, which is entirely free of the fungal spores found in virtually all samples of hay. The compact quarter-size bagged bales are also economical on space, which can be at a premium when travelling. The product does not keep well once the bag is open and must be used within two days.

Tying rings are necessary to secure your horse. Tie up as short as possible, with only just enough length of rope to allow it to eat the hay. If it has too much rope, there is always a risk that it might try to turn round, or get its head behind the upright of the partition. Tying fairly high (your horse's eye level) is generally reckoned to be safest, but colts sometimes try to rear, so they can be safer tied up at chin level. A

It is safest to close the rear of the trailer until the youngster is used to travelling, in case the open back is seen as a way out.

Check that the ramp does not wobble. Here a block of wood ensures that it is level and wobble free — Debbie tests! Note that the sun is behind the trailer and lights its interior.

horse that insists on trying to turn, or to chew the rope, is best tied up on both sides, pillar-rein fashion. If the side rings of the headcollar are used, it is less able to get the ropes into the mouth. There is much debate as to whether or not to use a loop of string on the tie ring for safety. There is a good argument for not using a string which will break, for it may precipitate a fall or even allow the horse to flip over backwards if the string breaks should it rear (or try to). A leather headcollar can overcome the problem as it is safest and most comfortable, and will break under excessive pressure. Ideally, the rope should loop on to the headcollar or be fitted with a trigger clip. Spring clips can too easily get caught and have caused many serious injuries.

If using a trailer, it is best to close the back doors (or screen) above the ramp until the young horse has become used to travelling — the space may be too inviting if he decided he does not like his situation! Later, when this risk is deemed to have passed, the back doors can be left open (securely latched back, of course) to provide welcome and necessary ventilation, in all but the coldest winter months.

Allow plenty of time for loading up. Choose your spot carefully. It is best if you can pull forward and straight to commence the journey directly. If the first experience of a journey is one of shunting backwards and forwards, the horse may get very disorientated and so not travel as well as it might. Unless you have a purpose-built loading bay (and most of us don't!) try to find a position where the ground is rising under the ramp. This will reduce its angle slightly. It is safer to load up on grass in case the horse slips, falls or plays up. If this is not possible, the yard will have to suffice. Sweep up droppings immediately, however, as they can make otherwise non-slip concrete treacherous. Parking next to a building reduces the lines of exit, but watch out for the danger posed by windows, gutters, doors and so on. Fences and hedges are very hazardous for both the horse and the handler. You are frankly better off without them than risking injury as you or the horse (or you both) crash into them. Always load in an enclosed area. Close all gates to roads and fields. Never load or unload a young or inexperienced horse on a highway.

Horses' eyes are in many ways better than ours – they can see more in low light conditions than we can, for instance, but they take much longer to adjust to different levels of light. If the inside of the box is in shade, the contrast to this from sunlight may be so much as to appear as a black void to the horse. Position the box so that the sun shines into it, with the sun behind the horse as it goes in. It then won't be dazzled and can see where it is going. Lowering the other ramp or opening the groom's door will also admit more light.

It may be correct to load a horse using a bridle or lunge cavesson, but if your youngster has never been bitted or worn a cavesson, it may make it harder, not easier, to handle. If it is very strong and trouble is anticipated, get it used to a bridle or lunge cavesson beforehand, or use a restraining halter for loading. Otherwise, use a fully adjustable headcollar and make sure it is fitted firmly. Load up using an extra long rope, so if it does play up it is less likely to get away. A lunge rein is also suitable, but rope gives better grip. Wear gloves, a hard hat and strong footwear. Make the box look as inviting as possible, with plenty of space for the horse to get in, the haynet already tied in and the bedding laid on the floor and the ramp. It will be even more inviting if the straw came out of its own stable and smells familiar (it is not necessary to include muck – just the fact that it has been near its droppings will be enough).

Young horses are not used to leg protection, and in any case their slim legs and small feet result in travel wraps or bandages slipping very easily. If you take good care and the horse box is well made and safe, it may be better not to use bandages or wraps. Should they slip on the journey, an inexperienced horse may panic, lashing out wildly and causing serious damage. It is not safe to enter a confined space, such as that for travelling, with any horse, let alone a young one and certainly not for the purpose of refitting leg protection. Young, slender legs with small hooves offer very little resistance to slipping travel boots or bandages, adding to the problems of wrapping their legs safely.

Bribery is essential when boxing! A tasty snack to reward good behaviour helps to get the message across and keep the youngster happy. Use some of the usual feed or sliced apples

The trailer is ready for Jaz's first loading. Ramp steady and level; partition moved across for extra space; straw everywhere! The front ramp is up but the door open to admit light. The haynet is safely tied up.

or carrots if you know they are enjoyed. Put the food in a bucket, but one without a handle, so should it get in the way or get dropped, there is no chance that the legs could get injured by getting caught up in it. Your task may be even easier if the horse is just a little hungry.

With everything ready, the yard gate shut and an assistant on hand, you are ready to start loading up. *Know* your horse *will* box and approach the whole thing with this positive attitude. Your progress even to approaching the ramp might be slow, but make sure that, even if your baby horse does not actually step forward, it is not going backwards, pulling or running away. Once you are up to the ramp, it may not be able to work out how to step up on to it. This is the time to keep very calm, stop it from going backwards and quietly pick up a forefoot and place it on the ramp. It may be necessary to move all the feet in turn, but as you do each one, quietly encourage it to walk on, if it feels confident enough to do so. Usually once it has a hind foot on the ramp, you'll find the pupil will then carry on and walk the rest of the way into the box unaided.

A companion horse at this stage can help, but it will need to be a very quiet and patient horse who will not start banging and shouting if it gets bored or thinks it is missing out on the action with regard to edible rewards!

If a companion is to be used to help the novice, then it must be the one to be boxed first. However, unboxing must be considered from the outset, because if the layout of the box is such that the first to load must be the first to unload, you could have a nasty situation with the youngster panicking as the companion disappears. In most lorries, there should not be a problem in removing the youngster first if it loaded last. If using a trailer with a front ramp for unloading, it is usually best to remove the horse from the ramp side first, so that the partition can be swung over to give the horse on the far side room to make the tighter turn to the ramp. Trailers which have only one ramp, down which the horse has to back in order to unload, should not be used for young horses. So, if using a trailer, or a lorry with a similar layout, load the companion first, on to the side away from the ramp.

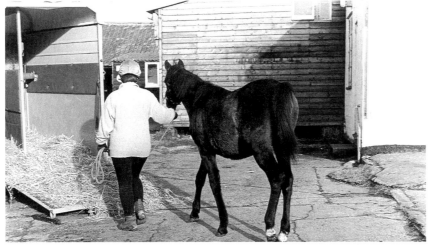

Yearling Jaz is led up to the box calmly and confidently. Debbie looks ahead. Note extra long rope, gloves, hat, stout footwear. A grass surface is ideal, but in winter, as here, a firmer surface has to do. No obstructions or obstacles are on the yard.

Jaz pauses to inspect the new object. Debbie remains calm and her attitude invites Jaz to step forward.

Within seconds, Jaz steps on to the ramp, cautious but confident in her handler.

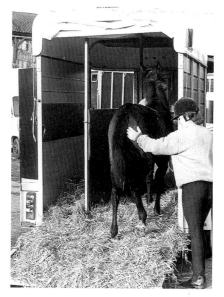

Dawn is ready to encourage Jaz to complete her journey. Again, note the safe clothing.

As soon as Jaz is safely installed, Dawn closes the ramp. She is safely positioned at the side. Jaz is being very good in spite of apparent anxiety!

Jaz is now tied up fairly short to the outer wall of the trailer. She cannot get her head past the upright of the central partition. Note the correctly fitted headcollar with 'proper' buckles and all ends neatly tucked in. Debbie remains at her head whilst all is made safe. Remember it is illegal as well as unsafe to travel in a trailer.

Dawn fastens the ramp on Jaz's side as soon as it is up. She remains safely to the side. The other side is fastened next. The ramp has been raised before re-arranging partitions.

Dawn now secures the partition which had been moved across to allow more room for loading. Talking gently while doing this prevents the youngster from getting alarmed.

The reasons for loading the older horse first are that it will set an example to the inexperienced youngster and you are in a position to put the ramp up as soon as the youngster is in, preventing any risk of it trying to get out again backwards.

Once in, close the ramp quickly and quietly with no delay. Continue feeding to keep it calm, and if in a lorry do up the partitions, talking to the horse all the time so it knows where you are. Remove the bridle, cavesson or restraining halter if one of these was used, tie it up, loosen the noseband of the headcollar, then check round to make sure everything is safe. If this is just a rehearsal, let it stand in the box for a few minutes, then take it out again. Give it plenty of time to see what it has to do and to work out how to come down the ramp. Use your long rope again. Keep at the shoulder, so if it does rush or jump, you won't get trodden on or knocked over. An older, more experienced horse brought up the ramp of a lorry and turned at the top to 'escort' the novice down can ensure that unboxing is achieved calmly and can avert a tendency to leap from the top of the ramp. Never rush or hassle the youngster out.

(*Left*) For Jaz's first time, she has not had a journey and is unboxed after a short time during which she was quite calm and enjoyed a reward. For unloading, the breast bar has been removed and the partition swung across to make a safe exit. Debbie leads her calmly forward. Note the straw on the ramp.

(*Right*) Be ready for a young horse to spring out. Debbie has remained safely at Jaz's shoulder and kept her on the ramp. On these occasions, you can be glad of a long rope and safe clothing.

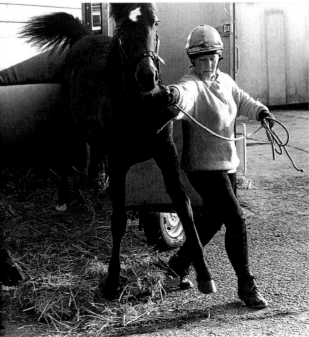

Safely hitched and ready to go: safety cable attached; lighting wiring has sufficient slack to allow for cornering but no more; hand brake is off; jockey wheel is fixed in the up position.

A confident, well handled and correctly disciplined young horse should not be any trouble to load the first, or subsequent times. If sufficient time is taken so there is no atmosphere of rushing or panic, and the vehicle is solid, safe and gives a good ride, it is perfectly reasonable to undertake a journey straight away. If there has been a flaw in the young horse's training, or it is particularly nervous, then repeated rehearsals may be necessary before travelling.

Over-practising can be detrimental, especially with a bright youngster. If the apparent reason for loading into the box or trailer is merely to come out again, it will not be long before its response is to refuse to go in. This first refusal may well be the very time when you need to undertake a real journey, perhaps for your first show. The previous pointlessness of the exercise, combined with the air of expectancy, even nervousness, that the handler will inevitably create, may be enough to persuade the horse that this is the day he objects.

Whenever a horse is to be travelled, ensure that it starts off calm. Horses are very sensitive to atmosphere, and rush, bustle, raised voices and any suggestion of panic in its human leaders could well start ringing alarm bells for the horse. The horse will not know it is going to a show, unless it is told!

If the journey is 'for real', you will of course have checked lights, oil, water, fuel, tax disc, tyre pressures and all the rest that is necessary before taking any vehicle out on the road.

Drive very carefully and even more slowly than you thought you'd need to! If you are towing a trailer, remember that the wheelbase of the trailer is likely to be wider than that of the car you are towing with so keep an eye on your nearside wing mirror to make sure you are not clipping the kerb, or dropping the trailer's nearside wheels in potholes or drain gratings at the side of the road.

Allow twice as much distance as usual for slowing down at traffic lights, junctions and roundabouts. Ease the brake pedal as you stop to avoid jolting your precious cargo. Slow down before bends, not as you go into them, and save accelerating away until you are on the straight again. Steady, defensive driving in this way will considerably reduce the stress of travelling for your horse.

When you reach your destination, don't be in a rush to unload. Habits created when young are hard to alter later on. A horse which will wait patiently until you are ready is much easier to manage than the one that starts yelling and stamping as soon as you arrive, demanding to be let out because it had always been unloaded as soon as it arrived on previous occasions. If the journey has disturbed the horse, it will help restore its confidence if it is allowed to settle on arrival. If it is unloaded as soon as the jolting stops, it may be reluctant to re-load to go home, the last association with the box being one of discomfort. A small feed on arrival will help make this last association with the box an enjoyable one.

Long journeys need breaking. It is very tiring for young legs to be braced and balancing, so stop for ten to fifteen minutes every couple of hours. Offer water, check the haynet and tying rope and generally offer the horse some comfort. The thought of a leg-stretch is nice for us, but it is not worth the risk on a motorway service area! If it is a very long journey, arrange a decent over-night stop in a roomy stable. We've all heard of the very long journeys race or competition horses undertake – aeroplanes can't stop in mid-Pacific! But just because some horses *have* to keep going doesn't mean it is the *best* way to travel. Give the horse the same breaks as you give the driver, then both will finish the journey in good condition. For journeys of more than 24 hours EC rules with regard to resting, feeding and watering are applicable, but most owners would want many more frequent stops than those require.

Although many horses are travelled in trailers which nearly always carry the horse facing forwards in the direction of travel, it has been shown that horses in fact travel better, with measurably lower levels of stress, facing the back.

Mares with foals are usually travelled loose, so they uniquely have the opportunity to choose the way they face. In my experience, the mares invariably position themselves facing the back, or diagonally across the box, facing the rear. The foals tend to stand alongside, or lie down. Other researchers have also found that facing the rear is the direction of choice, and have even found stress levels to be up to one-tenth of those recorded from horses travelling facing forwards.

The reasons for this are not fully understood, but as it is such a repeatable phenomenon, it must be worthy of consideration. Given the choice, it must be better to travel a young horse facing the rear, either directly, or at an angle, as in a herringbone configuration horse box.

On any journey, it is sensible to make sure that you have enough feed, hay and water, not only for the planned trip but also for any unplanned delay due to a breakdown. An extra net of hay should suffice, but why do so many people going to shows hang their spare hay on the outside of the lorry? It risks getting wet and spoiled should it rain, it is mopping up diesel fumes and lead pollution and, in addition, swinging haynets are a hazard to over-taken cyclists. Keep your spare hay inside. If you use haylage which comes in plastic wrapped bales, storage is no problem — each bale is one quarter the size of the equivalent hay bale.

Finally, however good your youngster's companion is, do not forget that it, too, will need care and attention, which will include some form of exercise. A seasoned travelling companion will help the youngster overcome the inevitable stresses of travelling, but, however experienced it may be, it, too, is under stress and has a need for considerate care.

The grey four year old will be an experienced and familiar travelling companion for any of these yearlings.

14 ROUTINE SERVICING

Just as a car needs an oil change every 6,000 miles and a full service every 12,000, so there are certain routine procedures necessary to keeping your horse in good order.

All horses should be vaccinated at least for tetanus and preferably for influenza as well. Some vets also recommend vaccination for rhinopneumonitis, an annoying cold-type virus which is responsible for keeping many racehorses at home. Foals may have had an anti-tetanus shot soon after they were born, but vaccination proper does not start until the youngster is over three months old. The first two shots can be combined flu and tetanus. They are given around four weeks apart, but can be within the range of 21−90 days to comply with the Jockey Club regulations, which apply to all horses on race-course property, not just for racing but for shows, club events and camps. The third shot, which is given around six months after the second, will be for flu only. This injection must be given within the range of 150−210 days after the second. From then on, boosters are normally given not more than one year apart. Tetanus is necessary only in alternate years, but many vets give the combined dose each time. The vaccination record must be completed by the veterinary surgeon each time. The batch number of the vaccine and its type are entered, and then it is signed and stamped by the veterinary surgeon. Not only does the certificate carry all this information, but it also has an identity chart to record the horse's colour, markings, freeze brand and so on, so there is no doubt as to what animal it refers.

All horses get worms and all horses need worming, but

young horses are particularly susceptible to a wide range of worms, many of which do not trouble older horses. Generally, horses do not acquire much immunity to worms, but mature horses are rarely troubled by threadworm (*Strongyloides westerii*) which is a particular pest of foals, causing scouring. Not all wormers are effective against this and those that are may need an increased dose rate. Youngsters under twelve months should be treated for this worm.

Roundworms (ascarids) are rarely found in horses over four years old, but can be a serious problem with yearlings and, to a lesser extent, two year olds. The eggs of this worm remain viable on the pasture or even in the stable for up to five years so it is important to treat for these worms throughout the horse's growing period to reduce to a minimum the chance of eggs being produced to infect another youngster in years to come. Most wormers will treat these ascarids at normal dose rates, but check your wormer each time – some require a double dose for full effectiveness. The most usual roundworm of horses is *Parascaris equorum*. The horse picks up the worm as eggs from the pasture or the stable. Larvae hatch out and from the small intestine roundworm larvae migrate to the youngster's lungs, where they cause coughing. They return to the mouth with the mucus from the lungs, then are re-swallowed and from the stomach continue to the small intestine again, and egg-laying maturity. A pot-bellied foal or yearling with a cough is very likely to be suffering from a roundworm infestation.

Worming is very important in young horses. These examples were from a six-month-old foal wormed seven weeks after the last dose, so was three weeks overdue. The dung bolus has small redworm (small, thin, white-looking worms); the red maggot is a bot; the larger specimen is an ascarid (white round worm). Full-grown examples of these can be twice as long and twice as thick.

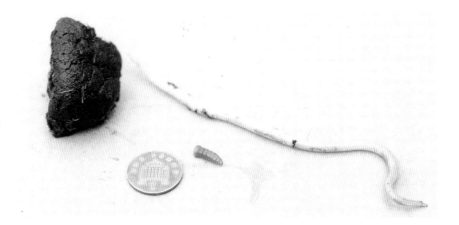

Redworm, members of the *Strongyle* family, infest all horses at all ages. They are picked up as larvae, usually from the pasture, but can also be picked up in the stable. They can be very damaging, as they migrate in the larval stages throughout the horse's body, using blood vessels as a kind of motorway system. No major organ is entirely safe from the ravages of this pest. Untreated, two year olds are likely to show the worst effects, being very anaemic, emaciated with a terrible coat and dreadfully lethargic. They will never fully recover from a bad dose of redworm. There are two main types, large and small redworm. Adults are found in the large intestine.

All worm medicines should be effective against adult redworm at a standard dose rate. Some are also effective against migrating redworm. Unfortunately, some drugs, those in the Benzidiazole family, whose names generally end in -zole, are no longer always effective against small redworm as the worms have in some cases become resistant to this chemical and members of its family. It is unfortunate that these small redworm are the most numerous of the worms burdening horses, accounting for up to 95 per cent of the worm eggs in an inadequately wormed horse's droppings.

Such wormers should not be relied upon for the treatment of small redworm, but some have useful activity against, for instance, *Strongyloides westerii* so need not be totally eliminated from the worming programme.

Tapeworm is increasingly recognised as a problem in horses, and is especially prevalent on old pasture as opposed to new leys. Only one drug (Pyrantel) is effective, and that only at double the standard rate of use. Tapeworm are found mainly at the junction of the small and large intestines, and can interrupt the flow of digesting food through the ilio–caecal valve. Affected horses may fail to thrive and can be prone to recurrent bouts of colic, each bout in itself not severe, but worrying because of the sometimes frequent recurrence. The problem has only recently been fully understood, and may have become more prevalent as modern wormers and effective worming regimes remove an increasing proportion of the rest of the worm burden, which may be in competition with the tapeworms.

After worming, examine the dung from 20 to 48 hours after dosing. A few small worms are visible on the surface of the boluses of this dung from a two year old, wormed 22 hours previously. The presence of worms shows that the wormer used was effective, but also suggests that the last wormer was not, or that too long an interval has elapsed. If no worms are seen, do not suppose there were none – you may have missed them.

Horses pick up worms mainly from contaminated pasture, but stables are not always the 'safe' place you might think. Deep litter bedding can allow worms to develop, and if the horse is fed from the floor (either deliberately or because it spilt food from its manger and ate it up later) the risk of picking up worms becomes a reality. Roundworm eggs will stick wherever the muck touched. Foals pick them up from the walls during exploratory nibbles round the stable. Redworm are picked up as larvae which become infective around ten days after the dropping containing the eggs was produced. By this time, the larvae can be up to ten metres away from the dung and will be situated in a water droplet (such as dew) on a blade of grass until eaten by a grazing horse. Only very thorough, daily dung removal will have any effective control, and even then is not totally effective. Weekly removal of droppings from the field is a waste of time. Moving the horse to new pasture at the same time as worm dosing is better. The field can be harrowed to break the dung and allow the sun and air to kill the worms. Horses should not be returned to a harrowed field for at least three weeks to allow time for the vast majority of the worm larvae to die a harmless death.

Horse worms are killed by the digestive systems of cattle, sheep and goats, and their worms are killed by the horse's digestive system. There is one exception only, the stomach hair worm. Luckily it is pretty rare! Grazing with different species can help worm control. Donkeys, being equids, share the same worm species. Additionally, they are prone to lung-worm. Most donkeys have this, but show few signs of it, being able to tolerate it with little apparent ill effect. Horses picking up lungworm are much more seriously affected by it, becoming run down with a persistent cough. If donkeys are kept with horses, effective lungworm treatment for all the horses and donkeys should be included in the worming pro-gramme. Some products require large, multiple doses.

Whatever other system is used, there is no getting away from the fact that all horses will need treating for worms frequently and for life. This should be done every month from one month of age until eighteen months, then every six weeks (or every eight weeks if you are fortunate enough to have extensive and well-managed grazing) for the rest of the horse's days. It is wise to use, as routine, a product with no known resistance problems. In spring and autumn, dose for tapeworm. Between December and March, one of the doses could be with a product which will also kill bots, insect larvae which live in the stomach. In the summer they develop into those annoying horse flies which lay eggs on the horse's legs, shoulders and mane. Using something to kill migrating worms mid-summer and when the horses are stabled for the winter will also help prevent a build-up. All horses sharing the same pasture should be dosed at the same time.

Wormers come as paste or powder. The paste is designed to be squirted into the horse's mouth. It sounds a really good idea, but is not always easy with a youngster who may resent the interference. If the mouth is empty before you start, what goes in, stays in, but if there is some food, for instance on the back of the tongue or against the molars, this can be spat out, taking the expensive wormer with it! It can be more satisfactory all round if the wormer is mixed with some soaked sugar beet (provided the horse is accustomed to being fed on this) which is then mixed into his usual feed. Very, very few horses will fail to take wormer this way; if the food has been eaten, you can be certain all the worm dose has reached its destination. Powders (and granules) will of course be fed by this method anyway. Do not try to mix worm powders directly with nuts alone — it doesn't work. Get some sugar beet soaked, give a little every day for three or four days to get the horse used to it, then mix in the wormer. In-feed worming, correctly carried out and supervised to ensure it has all been taken, is effective and stress free, with no wastage or risk of injury.

Wormers are potentially dangerous drugs and their distribution is carefully controlled. Only registered, qualified retailers are allowed to sell them. The same care should be taken following their purchase. They should be kept in a secure place and a record kept of products bought, used, effects and dates. Some wormers are toxic to other species, not just intestinal parasites. Organophosphorous compounds are contained in some wormers effective against bots. This drug will also kill birds, who may peck up leftover or spilled food. Uneaten dosed food should not be fed to domestic fowl and certainly not to geese, to which it is highly toxic. Ivermectin, another drug effective against bots, is a powerful insecticide, not altered by the horse's digestive processes. Droppings containing it will be lethal to flies, dung beetles and other insects which are an important part of nature's cycle. The insects carry fungi and bacteria which rot the droppings.

On very well-managed systems, which include frequent resting of pastures and newly wormed horses going on to 'clean' pasture, it is possible to reduce worming intervals to once every two months. This can help reduce the adverse effects of worm dose products on the environment and can result in financial savings, too. It is wise occasionally to test the effectiveness of any worming programme by once or twice a year getting the vet to do a faecal worm egg count when the horses are due to be wormed. It is not necessary to test all the individuals in a large group; random sampling of, for instance, one in each age group would be sufficient, or one that does not look as well as the others.

The testing is done on a small sample of fresh dung. Using a microscope, the worm eggs in the prepared specimen are counted and the number present in one gram of dung is calculated. This number is the 'worm count'. Under 200 is considered low; 500 suggests that worming is overdue or the last dosing was to some extent ineffective; higher counts on dosed horses indicate that worming has been ineffective and that the worms are resistant to the product used.

Another important routine is farriery. A shod horse needs its shoes replaced at least every six weeks. Even if the shoes are not worn, the feet will need trimming. It helps to remember both shoes and worming if you do them both at the same time, as they both need doing at six-weekly intervals.

However, the vast majority of young horses are not shod. As they are not doing road work, shoes should not be necessary. Also, shoes increase the risk of splints developing, either from knocks from the opposite foot or due to the extra concussion caused by the additional weight of iron. Without shoes, the

It is important that the horse is well used to its feet being handled before asking the farrier to trim it. Debbie holds the horse correctly, on the same side as Steven Taylor, and facing the horse and farrier.

feet wear naturally to a certain extent, so unless the farrier is attending more frequently to sort out a problem, a visit from him every twelve weeks should be sufficient. Before the farrier comes, however, make sure that you can handle your youngster's feet and legs and that it has learnt a few basic manners. It will have to stand on three legs a lot longer for the farrier than for you when you pick out the hooves. It is fair on neither the farrier nor the horse if it is not prepared for the experience. The farrier could get injured and the horse could get frightened. If the horse is owned and handled only by women and this bad experience is its first close encounter with a man, the horse can gain the reputation for hating men. It is not the fault of the male farrier, but your fault for not preparing it sufficiently for the experience.

Your young horse must learn to stand with patience while routine tasks are carried out. An important part of this is learning to be tied up for gradually increasing lengths of time. Your vet or farrier will appreciate the good manners which will enable their task to be done more quickly, efficiently and safely for all concerned.

One routine procedure occurs once in the life of the majority of colts. It is castration, or gelding. Some vets will do this at your own premises, others prefer to admit the colt. It is not an operation which should be delayed. If your colt is not destined for a stud career, the sooner it is gelded, in most cases, the better. Colts which are gelded as foals cause the least trouble and an increasing number of vets are happy to perform this surgery even prior to weaning.

Whilst official stud duties cannot start until a colt is at least twenty-four months old, nature has not read the rule book and it is quite possible for a yearling colt to perform as a stallion with fertile results. Similarly, yearling fillies are capable of conceiving. For this reason, if none other, it is sensible to castrate colts before their hormones start to surge, which is usually in the spring of their first birthday. The sights and sounds of in-season mares and fillies can turn a docile and easy to handle youngster into a boorish, noisy, nippy and thoroughly difficult adolescent. Once this has happened, most vets will refuse to operate until the autumn, however much you protest. The risk of flies spreading infection into the wound is high. Keeping the horse stabled to keep it away from the flies slows healing and greatly increases the amount of swelling.

Testosterone (the male hormone produced in the testes) is responsible for the behavioural changes seen in a colt or young stallion. It may also give the colt more presence and a more muscled physique which you might want for the show ring, if that is more important to you. Once castrated, the male tendencies are gradually lost — temperament, physique and character all gradually become like any other gelding's. But the later the operation is done, the longer these changes take and the greater the risk of some habits becoming ingrained as vices. For instance, a late-cut colt may lose his cresty neck, but may not lose the tendency to nip, if this has become an almost reflex action or a habit.

If the castration takes place after the colt's maleness is obvious, the operation has a far more profound effect. For a start, there is more to remove the more developed the youngster has become. The larger the horse, the more anaesthetic is required. The new gelding will also have to cope with the sudden cessation of testosterone, a hormone which, among other things, will create a feeling of well being. In a word, he will feel depressed following the operation and the older he is the more depressed he will feel post-operatively. His arrogant superiority as a stallion has been removed from him at a stroke.

Although a routine operation, castration is, nevertheless, major surgery and as with any surgery there are risks involved. The actual surgery itself is always the same; both testicles are removed via an incision in the scrotum. An instrument called an emasculator is used, which crushes rather than cuts the tubes and blood vessels leading to the testicle. They are removed one at a time. Although the blood vessels may be sutured to prevent bleeding, the incisions are usually left open to allow the wound to drain. There is bruising which will cause con-

Castration is a necessary procedure for most colts. Here Je'phari is being 'cut' under a general anaesthetic at home. The veterinary nurse is holding the emasculator, which crushes rather than cuts, reducing bleeding. Charlotte holds the hind leg to expose the operation site. The vet is checking the administration of anaesthetic.

siderable swelling if the new gelding does not get sufficient, gentle exercise after the operation.

The operation can be carried out under sedation only, with the colt standing, or with a general anaesthetic and the colt recumbent. The choice usually depends on the vet's preference and the place where the operation takes place.

If general anaesthetic is to be used, the colt is usually starved of solid food for up to twenty-four hours prior to the operation. This is not necessary if a sedative only is used.

Although many vets prefer to perform castrations at their own surgeries, some will do them 'in the field', in other words at the colt's usual home. Assisting in such circumstances, as in any operation, can be a fascinating experience, if you are able to cope with it. The vet will need a suitable area to perform in, which could be a large, clean, well-bedded stable (straw rather than shavings) or a safely enclosed paddock. If the colt is to have a general anaesthetic, a towel is needed to place under its head to protect the eye. An opened-out feed bag can be used to tuck under the flank and stifle, to prevent dirt or bedding getting into the wound. The vet will need a table (or a straw bale) on which to place his instruments safely clear of the horse, and a couple of buckets of warm water, soap and towel. A disposal bag is also required.

When the youngster comes round, it will need twenty or thirty minutes of gentle walking in hand — the vet will enjoy a cup of tea! If it is cold at night, it may be better to stable the gelding the first night. The stable should previously have been scrubbed, disinfected and lavishly bedded with straw. In mild weather and certainly all day, the horse should be in a safely fenced, small, sheltered paddock with a steady companion. There may be some exudate or blood on the legs which will need cleaning off, but the vet will have protected the horse against infection with antibiotics. If all has gone well with no complications, infection should not be a problem, but swelling will be, if there is insufficient exercise. A healthy gelding will be healed up and fully recovered in around two weeks, but a late-cut, mature colt may not be completely fit again for up to six weeks.

15 TEETH

Riding horses generally have their teeth checked regularly, perhaps annually when the vaccination boosters are given, for instance. It is not common practice to rasp a youngster's teeth, however. Firstly, they rarely get trouble with their milk teeth. Secondly, rasping can be an unnerving experience for a horse which has never even had a bit in its mouth. But occasionally dental care is indicated. Sometimes, a yearling might look a bit like a hamster with wads of food collected in one or both cheeks. If this is associated with a loss of condition, or you notice that it does not spend as much time grazing as other horses do, it may need its molars rasped. Teeth which are crowded are uneven; uneven teeth soon become sharp teeth.

Although rasping away the sharp bits is very straightforward, there is every chance it could be upsetting, so it may be advisable to sedate the horse before the vet even starts. Modern effective sedatives are given intravenously, so they can legally only be administered by a qualified veterinary surgeon. The farrier, dental technician or the local 'tooth man' is not suitably qualified and should not be employed in this instance. Some vets and other horse teeth specialists like to remove the worn-out crowns of the milk molars from three year olds. There is not usually any problem with shedding these milk teeth — in fact, they frequently turn up in the mangers of 2½–3½ year olds! Removal of them may prevent any possible setback if eating is uncomfortable whilst they are being shed naturally. Unless the youngster is 'quidding' or losing weight, there is not likely to be a problem, and removing these crowns is

The bulge in one-year-old Jamborino's cheek is due to a wad of grass caught on uneven molars. These will need rasping.

completely unnecessary. Quidding involves the horse dribbling or spilling from the mouth chewed wads of food and is considered a clear indicator of dental discomfort.

Once identified, sharp teeth should be treated promptly. The sharp teeth can lacerate the tongue or the insides of the cheek and even set up painful ulcers in these areas. Eating is usually seriously curtailed once this happens. Condition is always so much harder to put back on a growing horse than it is to lose.

Bad breath in horses, as in people, can be an indicator of a problem in the mouth. This is not always the teeth, however. The sharp awns of barley grass, for instance, can lodge in the gums or the insides of the cheeks and lips. This can cause a painful, infected and sore area. It is easily remedied by removing the offending awn or seed with your fingers or some tweezers, and then sponging the horse's mouth out with plenty of salty water. Barley grass grows in old meadows. Grazing horses generally avoid it, but it can be a problem if it is in the hay or keep is short on the grazing, forcing the horses to eat grasses they would normally avoid.

This barley grass looks pretty but its awns can damage gums.

As with other mammals, horses have two sets of teeth. The milk, or deciduous, teeth are smaller, whiter and smoother than the permanent teeth. They also have much smaller roots. The teeth are of very distinct types. The incisors are highly specialised nippers for grazing. There are six at the front of each jaw. The numbers are the same for both milk and permanent teeth. The canine teeth, which are especially well developed in carnivores, for tearing flesh, are all but lost in horses. There are no milk canines, and only males develop permanent canines, known in horses as tushes. They are halfway along the gap between the incisors and the molars in each jaw.

Horses have premolars and molars, but as they have developed to look and function the same, are all conveniently referred to as molars. There are three in each side of each jaw in the milk set, and six in the permanent set. Some horses get 'wolf teeth' which are small, rudimentary, shallow-rooted premolars, found just in front of the molars in the upper jaw. Contact between these useless teeth and the bit can be painful, so they are routinely removed in most cases as soon as they are identified.

The upper jaw is wider than the lower, so the molars do not appear to match up, but they should wear evenly due to the sideways movement of the lower jaw during mastication. This grinds food as well as crushing it. This grinding is essential if the horse's natural, rough, fibrous diet is to be able to travel down the oesophagus. The front teeth should match up perfectly, each tooth in line with its partner in the opposite jaw.

Misalignments of the front teeth are a serious problem. The most common fault is parrot mouth. The lower jaw is apparently not long enough, and the top incisors overhang those in the lower jaw. A horse with this problem may not be a very effective grazer, so will not 'do' as well at grass as it ought. A stabled diet does not pose the same problems for it, however. More importantly, the back teeth are likely also to be out of alignment, the upper and lower teeth failing to match up longitudinally. Hence the first upper molars and last lower molars will fail to wear evenly, and will develop sharp points on them. These will need rasping if the sharp spikes are not to cause damage to the inside of the horse's mouth. This will need doing every four to six months throughout the life of the horse. Parrot mouth is considered to be an hereditary defect. Examination for this fault is part of the veterinary surgeon's examination on behalf of a purchaser, and, unless very slight, will result in the animal failing. It is also heavily penalised in the show ring.

The opposite of parrot mouth is monkey mouth (or hog's jaw). It is very much rarer, but the points mentioned above all apply equally. The sharp points on the molars will form on the first molars in the lower jaw, and the back-most upper molars.

A young horse's age can be estimated from its teeth, as they all tend to appear to a fairly regular timetable. A mal-nourished youngster may be backwards in its teeth as well as in its body development; conversely, some youngsters seem to come from families which are quick maturing and are ahead of their chronological age in their teeth.

Ages at which milk teeth are cut

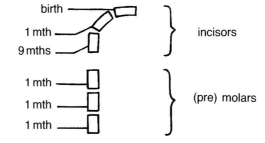

Ages at which permanent teeth are cut

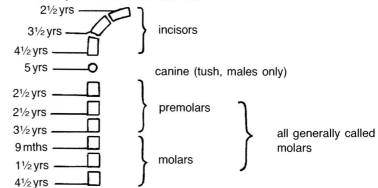

Table of teeth. Diagrams represent one half of one jaw.

A foal is born with its front central teeth, two in the centre of each jaw. If not actually visible, they can be felt just under the skin, and will cut through soon after birth. In the next four weeks, the adjoining teeth, the lateral incisors, will come through. The set of milk incisors will be complete at nine months, when the corners appear. The biting surface (tables) of these corners will not match up with each other over the full width of the tooth until the horse is two years old.

Meanwhile, the molars have been developing. All the milk molars are through by the time the foal is a month old, then, at nine months, the first of the permanent molars comes through, one in each side of each jaw, immediately behind the rows of three milk molars. This coincides with the foal's fine and pretty head beginning to look heavier and larger, as the head has had to grow to accommodate these larger teeth. The second permanent molar in each side of each jaw is in use soon after emerging at one and a half years, and as it grows to its full size, can be responsible for a considerable lump in the lower jaw, which will be joined by a second 'tooth bump' the following year as the rest of the molars develop, ready to emerge by the time the horse is three and a half years of age.

Three-year-old Arab filly Kassya's jaws are almost bursting with teeth — even the upper jaw — note the bump below the eye and the 'wavy' outline of the lower jaw.

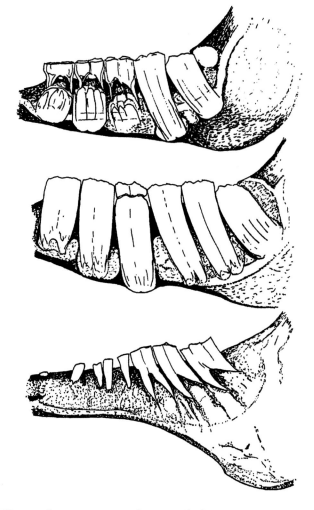

These diagrams taken from X-rays show equine jaws at different ages. (*Top*) Yearling, with all the milk teeth still in use, and the permanent molars developing. (*Centre*) A three year old's jaw bursting with teeth. (*Bottom*) Forty-five years old, with only a few stumps remaining. (From Michael Schaffer, *An Eye for a Horse*, J. A. Allen)

The milk molars are not designed for prolonged use, and will wear out very quickly when grass is being eaten more. They will be dislodged by their permanent counterparts. The first two in each side of each jaw are shed at around two and a half years, and the last ones, at three and a half.

Geldings and stallions cut their tushes when they are around four and a half years old.

The gums will be sore when new teeth are coming through, and may even become slightly infected. This does not usually cause any problem, being localised and of a temporary nature, but the glands in the angle of the jaw can be slightly inflamed. The teething horse may be off its feed to a small extent, and

Derri, yearling Thoroughbred filly. Her jaws are still slender as her massive permanent molars have not yet developed.

Derri is now rising three years old. Her head looks heavier and her lower jaw is bulging with new molars.

can be fractious. It may become headshy, nippy, or awkward to lead. It may chew wood and a loose molar at feed time can give the impression that the horse is eating gravel!

Shed milk teeth can often be found in the manger, the water trough or even spat out over the stable door! They make an interesting souvenir of your horse's youth!

Be sympathetic and aware of the youngster's changing dentition. Tight headcollars, chains under the jaw and bits can all cause discomfort if not actual pain, and are best avoided until its mouth has settled.

16 LEARNING

Your horse may learn something new because you have made a deliberate effort to teach something. For instance, you might decide today is the day it learns to box up, or to have its tail washed for the first time. Sometimes, new things are hard for an inexperienced horse to cope with. Perhaps it sees a greater threat in a new situation than you had considered it presented or it cannot cope with the new problem at all.

If the horse is accustomed to meeting new challenges, however small they seem, it will gradually come to accept the fact that you are pretty daft, and ask it to cope with some crazy notions, but it is best to humour the human because boss seems quite pleased if one does!

Horses are definitely creatures of habit and would generally like everything to be the same every day. But youngsters are inquisitive and will often handle new situations better than an older horse. If new challenges become routine, there will be far less upset when genuine challenges have to be met later on, such as going to shows, behaving in crowds on sponsored rides, adjusting to a new home or whatever else arises.

We can present new challenges in the most simple ways that may seem to be almost insignificant to us, but will help an impressionable youngster along the road to accepting what is required with good grace and good manners.

From time to time, change your horse's stable. Obviously on a large yard, this is much easier, but it is a simple way of presenting a new situation with not too much trouble. If possible find stables with different approaches: up a step, down a step, sloping up or down to the doorway. Of course,

(*Opposite*) This fallen tree has had its branches removed to reduce the risk of injury, but the trunk remains, providing interest for the horses and a haven for insects. Many horses seem nervous of fallen trees and tree stumps, but not Clyde, an Anglo-Arab yearling, with his seven-year-old companion, Flyer.

145

Even a small log creates interest in an otherwise featureless paddock.

make sure that the stable is big enough and that the doorway is high and wide enough to prevent an injury. Once in a new stable, reward it with some hay and a pat, or even a feed if it seemed more difficult for the horse than you expected. But after that, treat the new stable as normal. Occasionally, a different stable can get any horse very flustered and cross. If he is very upset, it may be wise to shut the top door. If it is upset merely because it is different and not because there is anything dangerous or frightening, avoid the temptation to take it out immediately. It must learn to accept the things that you ask of it even if it does not like them. You, however, must ensure that your requests are not unreasonable or frightening. In particular, a youngster will become very distressed if separated from its companions. Solitary confinement is a hard and cruel punishment for a young herd animal.

It will do every young horse good to spend at least some of its youth turned out next to a busy road or railway line. Steady company and safe, secure fences are a must, but learning to ignore loud noises, hoots, flapping loads and fast-moving traffic is a valuable lesson which will enhance your safety when later you and your young horse are enjoying rides together.

The terrain of the field or meadow can be stimulating or boring. A flat, featureless field with a post and rail fence may be very safe, but it is also lacking in stimulation. Hedges and trees offer homes to birds, so with these our youngster can get used to birds flying up. They will also give it a good excuse to go for a gallop, which will help to develop strong, sound muscles, ligaments and bones. Strength and soundness will be further stimulated by undulating or hilly terrain, which will also improve or develop his balance. Banks and ditches will encourage agility, suppleness and athleticism − all pre-requisites for any aspiring eventer, show-jumper or dressage horse. Rabbit holes, overgrown fox earths and blind (invisible due to long grass etc.) ditches are, however, not a challenge, merely a hazard. The idea is to develop, not destroy our youngster!

The fallen tree, the brook bank, the shady oak − a little 'adventure playground' for three yearlings.

Jamborino is developing his balance and agility by playing in this ditch with Trimaroo. Although good for the youngsters, this treatment is not ideal for the ditch. Unless ditches are free from all hazards they should be fenced off.

Scrambling up and down this shallow bank will improve Jenerous' balance and agility.

If a stimulating environment is not naturally available, a lot can be done to make life more interesting. Poles, branches, telegraph poles and logs can all be gradually introduced and the youngster encouraged to walk over them. These are *not* jumps, merely variations in the going. If it does not understand that you want it to walk over them, lay a pole across the gateway, and let it follow its companion over it into the field so it understands what is required. Poles, puddles, muddy bits can all provide a challenge whilst letting the horse know that he can walk on different textures and, eventually, go without changing pace, shying or baulking.

So many of the things that cause problems when schooling a riding horse can be avoided by introducing new challenges whilst the youngster is developing. Horses that hate farm animals, won't go through water or shy at white lines in the road may all have had an over-protected childhood.

It is important not to go over the top with new experiences. The young horse's confidence must not be destroyed by your enthusiasm. Stick to one new thing at a time and probably not more than one major challenge a month so that the new things can become familiar before a further learning opportunity is met.

Anyone who has a dog is in the custom of taking it for a walk. With increasing numbers of young horses being owned by people who perhaps have only the one horse, horse walking is gaining popularity. Traditionally, young horses have, to an extent, been treated as somewhat of a nuisance, and were generally turned out to grow and develop until they reached an age when they could do something useful, e.g. be ridden. Owning a horse privately is an expensive exercise. In exchange for the expenditure involved, you, as owner, would hope to get some reward − the companionship of your horse, the challenge of developing and educating your horse and the reward of seeing it develop physically, mentally and emotionally. Taking your horse for walks can help fulfil all these aims. It can be especially beneficial where grazing and the opportunity to exercise at liberty is limited. Before setting out into the countryside it is necessary to have formed some rapport with, and discipline over, your youngster. Trusting and obedient, it should not give you problems.

At first, walks will be limited to a stroll around the stable yard, later in nearby fields or paddocks. Lots of neighing suggests the horse is feeling insecure. You have either done too much or it is dependent on a companion which has not joined your promenade. It is easier in this case to arrange for a

A group of yearlings on a stud, practising leading and standing together. Their handlers are trainees and are learning too. This schooling is essential for showing, but is also valuable education for any young horse.

friend to join you with the object of your youngster's yearnings, but you may feel you want to encourage some independence, so for short walks near to home you may go 'solo'. This will help to develop a bond of friendship between you and your horse, provided you do not discourage it by tackling too much, too soon. Always build up gradually, making haste slowly.

Young horses are spooky and reactive. Strong footwear will help protect your feet against treads and offer good grip. A hard hat is an excellent precaution; so are gloves and either an extra long rope or a lunge line. A whip is a sensible precaution especially with a colt — you may also prefer to wear long sleeves if it is nippy. Colts can get very strong, so you may need to use a bit. It should be a smooth straight bit, used with a combination (three-way) coupling to which the lead (or lunge) rein is attached. The three ends attach to the two bit rings and to the noseband. This will put some of the pressure on to the noseband so it is not all in the mouth. Although it is preferable not to have to bit a young horse, it is better to bit it and have control, than not to and have it discover that you are not as strong as it is.

It is not safe or sensible to walk youngsters on the road. Should they shy or get loose, the consequences to other road users (as well as to the horse) could be dire. Walking on the road will also put excessive wear on the feet, causing foot-soreness, and may concuss the legs to the point of unsoundness. If it seems essential to use the roads, for instance just a short stretch to gain access to a bridleway, then it will be safer if a steady horse is ridden ahead of the youngster to give a lead. It will block to a certain extent attempts to rush forwards, and should there be an accident, rather than run home through the traffic, it will hopefully stay with the older horse. Additionally, the ridden horse will set a good example and the rider, being higher, will have a better view of approaching traffic and more chance to slow it down if necessary.

A short safe stretch of farm road is a suitable place for a walk, as long as the horse has good strong feet.

Walks should not be too long and, as with any exercise, the time increased gradually. There are no hard and fast rules, but building up to an hour or so should be plenty for you both!

Whilst not usual in this country, to 'ride and lead' a young horse from an older, steady horse is a way of educating the youngster without the leg work of walking yourself. In America, it is called 'ponying' and with a suitable escort horse and in safe terrain (not busy roads) is probably a very satisfactory way of combining exercise and learning whilst getting the horse out and about.

Should the youngster be so unfortunate as to suffer an injury to the legs, it may well need bandaging. If this is to be its first introduction to bandaging, it could be upsetting for the horse, risks worsening its condition, and is potentially hazardous to the handler. It is better to have accustomed it to having its leg wrapped before the need arises. Baby horses have slender legs and little feet, so there is not a lot to stop many types of bandage or leg wrapping from slipping or even sliding right off. The best type of bandage to use on a young horse is a cohesive one such as Vetrap. These bandages are very light, elastic, and stick only to themselves. As they cannot slip, it is not necessary to use padding under them, as is needed with every other type of bandage, so long as they are not left on for more than an hour or so. Take care not to over stretch them as they go on, or they will be too tight and uncomfortable. After the first turn round the leg, the bandage sticks to itself, and even if you drop it, it will not come off or unwind.

Get the horse used to bandages on the forelegs before you start on the hinds. When they are on, let the horse get used to them in the stable for a few minutes, then take it for a short walk. At first, it will have a very strange gait, lifting the legs high and possibly striking out with them, but keep clear, keep walking and it will soon settle down and walk quite normally again.

Cohesive bandages are quite expensive, but, if they are not put on too tightly, or each layer pressed too closely on to the previous layer, they can be removed carefully and reused several times. They are excellent for holding dressings or

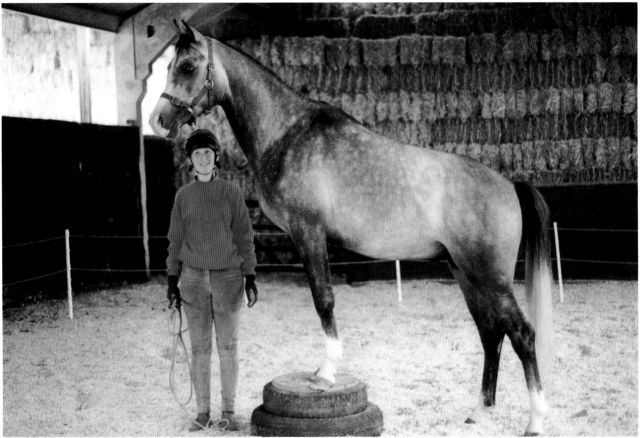

poultices in place, too.

You may be tempted to start schooling your horse for ridden work before it is three years old. Resist this temptation. It is easy to suggest quiet lunging, but it is not easy actually to do this with a green youngster which may have other ideas. Until the bones in the limbs have finished growing, permanent damage can result from an impatient start to work. Splints, windgalls, thoroughpins, bog spavin and strains are a possibility. Whilst recovery is likely from some of these, the soft swellings on or near the fetlocks from windgalls are there for life, as also are those on the hocks from bog spavin and thoroughpin.

Teach your horse plenty in hand, but do not rush and do not risk damage by putting it on to a circle before it is mature enough to withstand such a work load. It is possible that at

A suitable youngster may be prepared to try some less orthodox things: Justinus found learning circus tricks easy and it gave him a new interest as a rising three year old. Harmless and great fun!

shows you will see exuberant young horses being lunged, but this is not to say that such exercise is good for them. It is not in the best interests of a horse for which a long ridden career is planned. Very many successful young show horses fail to make the grade later, due in too many instances to unsoundness. Racehorses, bred and reared for two-year-old racing, are usually retired at four years. Little publicity is given to their enormous wastage rate. Only one in ten of the horses going into training ever wins a race, and this after half the eligible horses failed even to get as far as going into training in the first place.

A horse's soundness is a valuable and rarer commodity than many people realise. Around 70 per cent of riding horses offered for sale will fail the veterinary surgeon's suitability for purchase examination: in other words, will fail the vet due to unsoundness. A horse is 'vetted' only after a prospective purchaser has tried the horse, so the obviously lame ones will not have got as far as the vet's examination anyway. It all adds up to an awful lot of unsound horses and emphasises the need to take care not to impose extra stress and strain on an already vulnerable creature before it has any chance of being physically up to the task required of it.

Thoroughbred racehorses are backed whilst still yearlings and start their competitive flat racing career as two year olds. Most retire by the time they are four. Riding horses are best left longer to finish maturing. They are not bred to be quick maturing and are required to work for many more years.

17 MINOR AILMENTS

All young creatures seem to be accident-prone. Young horses are no exception and are susceptible to a wide range of minor, and sometimes not so minor, ailments and injuries.

Most injuries are avoidable. Young skin is thinner and more fragile than in maturity and the creature inside it not possessed of the sensibilities or cautiousness of age. Environmental hazards thus pose a greater threat to juveniles than to oldsters. However careful you are to avoid barbed wire, however clear of junk your yard and however apparently safe your fields and stable, it is almost inevitable that your young horse will suffer some sort of injury at some time. Very small wounds can be treated without the vet's help, but if the wound is more than one inch (2.5 cm) long and through all the skin layers, it will need the vet to stitch it, preferably within two hours of it happening and certainly within eight for a good chance of a successful outcome.

Large or rapidly filling swellings need veterinary attention as well as any injury causing lameness, as the risk of bone fractures may need investigation. Hurting horses are often frightened horses, and so not easy to treat. Most vets will choose to sedate an injured youngster before risking upsetting it further. Do not be alarmed at this but, rather, be grateful at the vet's concern for the animal's welfare.

For wounds to heal quickly and well, they must be kept clean, so take all your vet's advice on hygiene, keeping the horse and the stable as clean as possible. Muck out fully once a day; skip out several times in between. Use straw rather than woodchips. Woodchips adhere to wounds and con-

Even an innocent-looking tie ring like this can cause injury if you are unlucky.

(*Opposite*) Young horses, like young children, are more liable to pick up colds and runny noses. Jenerous, a yearling, has a slight discharge in both nostrils, white-to-clear; he is alert, his eyes bright, and where the whites show, they are normal, not bloodshot. No action necessary, but to be on the safe side, no shows until the snotty nose has cleared up.

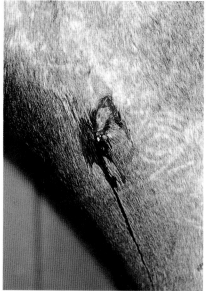

Youngsters are accident prone! This nasty tear-wound was caused in the stable, on the safe-looking, smooth tying ring shown on the previous page.

taminate them, delaying healing. Treatment will probably take place two or three times a day. This is when you will be especially glad that you taught the patient to tie up without fuss! Provided you can keep flies away from wounds, and the weather is suitable, they will probably heal better if the horse is turned out. The horse will also be calmer, more controllable and thus easier to treat, if it is following its usual routine as much as possible.

An injured horse is likely to be upset as well, so it is vital that you keep calm while investigating and treating wounds. The horse will quickly sense your distress which will increase its agitation and make it harder to treat. If you are the type who becomes emotional or nauseous in these circumstances, it may be better to recruit a level-headed, less involved assistant to take over from you.

There are various treatments which your vet might suggest that you carry out to assist the healing of a wound or injury. It is wise to be familiar with these before the need arises, and to have the necessary equipment available. You may even decide to practise some of them in advance, too.

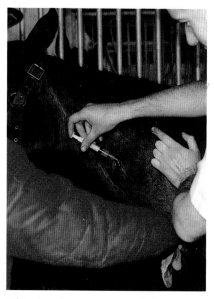

This is when you are glad your young horse has been well handled! The vet administers local anaesthetic —

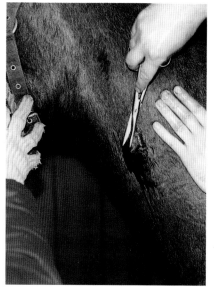

clips the hair away from the wound edges —

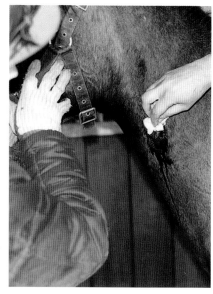

cleans it thoroughly —

COLD HOSING

Hosing with cold tap water is an effective way of cleaning a dirty wound. The cold water also chills the tissues, causing the capillaries to contract and thereby stemming minor bleeding. This effect will also help to reduce the impact of bruising, by limiting the amount of leakage into the area. It can prevent bruising from developing as much as it otherwise would have, and can reduce swelling on pre-existing injuries. Cold water hosing is usually carried out three or four times a day, for about twenty minutes each time. A firm, non-slip area should be chosen, with a drain and tap in close proximity. The area should be free from all hazards, as young horses being hosed are rarely quiet and may swing around a lot. Saturating the leg may cause cracked heels to develop, so before starting, protect the backs of the pastern and heel area with a layer of petroleum jelly. Use only a gentle flow of water, and start at the hoof, gradually working up the leg as the horse becomes accustomed to it. Gently squeeze your hand over the leg in the flow of water, to saturate the coat to the skin, so the hosing is as effective as possible. You will

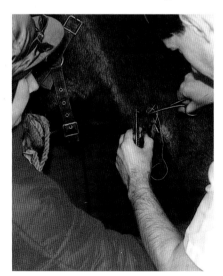

and stitches up. Note the handler sensibly wearing hat and gloves.

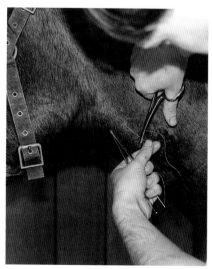

The skin is pliable, enabling the gaping hole to be closed up. This wound healed without leaving a scar.

Correct action taken promptly pays dividends – there is no sign of any scar on Justinus' neck (photo taken one year later).

almost inevitably need help to do this, even with a quiet horse. Although in theory any part of the horse could be cold hosed, in practice it is usually the limbs which receive this very useful treatment.

POULTICING

Poulticing is a good treatment for infected wounds, bruises, strains and sprains after three days of cold hosing. The heat of the poultice increases blood supply to the area, and assists the healing process. An absorbent, damp poultice will draw dirt and pus out of a wound or abcess. Animalintex is an excellent poultice whenever such a treatment is needed. It is a medicated cotton wool dressing, which is cut to size, saturated in boiling water, allowed to cool sufficiently to prevent scalding the horse, and applied under a layer of plastic, then bandaged over additional padding. Old fashioned, fiddly, messy, but cheap, a kaolin poultice can be very effective, too. The paste is warmed by standing the tin in a pan of boiling water. It will need stirring a couple of times to help it heat evenly. It is applied directly to the horse, your having first smeared the area with a thin protective layer of petroleum jelly. Cover the kaolin with gauze, and bandage in place with two layers of padding. If the skin is broken, the kaolin should be applied sandwiched between two layers of absorbent lint. Be very sure it is not too hot, as it holds a lot of heat and can give rise to a nasty burn. The poultice should be changed twice a day. After three days there should be considerable improvement and further poulticing should not be necessary, unless so directed by the vet. It is not practical to poultice the horse's body, but it is a useful treatment for injuries to the lower leg and the foot.

FOMENTING

Infected wounds and abscesses on the upper limbs or the body may look as if they would benefit from poulticing, but it is not practical or possible to apply a poultice. These are the instances when one would use fomenting as a treatment. An ounce (25 g) each of salt, Epsom salts and washing soda are dissolved in a pint (500 ml) of boiling water in a large plastic bowl, or a plastic bucket. This is then topped up to make a gallon (4 l) of hot, but not scalding, solution, using cold water and boiling water from the kettle. Wads of cotton wool are then squeezed out in this solution, and held against the affected area until cool. The pads should not be squeezed dry, but just enough to prevent too much surplus solution running down the horse. This is repeated for half an hour. As the solution cools, it is rewarmed by adding more boiling water from the kettle. If it is a wound or abscess being treated, or the skin is broken, each wad of cotton wool should be discarded when it is cool, and a new piece used. If there is no break to the skin, and no risk of infection, it can be more economical to use a folded piece of blanketing, which can be reused. Fomenting is performed three times a day, and is very good for drawing abscesses.

TUBBING

This treatment is so called because in former times a small oak tub was used. A solution is made up exactly as described above, in a large bucket without a handle. Tubbing is used to clean up badly contaminated wounds to the lowermost parts of the leg or foot, to draw puncture wounds and abscesses and to soften and draw the foot if there is an infection in it. Tubbing is more immediately effective than poulticing, while it is being done, but is time consuming. Having made the solution, the heels should be greased as for cold hosing, and the horse persuaded to stand with its foot in the bucket. Having gently eased the foot in, it can help the horse to keep it there if the opposite foot is lifted. This prevents the horse so easily from taking its foot out again. It may be necessary to cool the water to blood heat in order to get the horse to accept it at first, but then the temperature can be slightly increased by the addition of small amounts of hot water. Do not 'top up' with the foot in the bucket, for fear of scalding the horse. Keep up the treatment for up to half an hour if possible, and repeat it two or three times a day.

Worms are a problem for all horses but can have a more profound effect on young horses. A youngster looking off colour, lethargic, failing to thrive or just looking awful without any specific reason may well be wormy, but in case of something more sinister, it is wise to call the vet. A sick horse should not be wormed except under the veterinary surgeon's supervision. Worming is in itself stressful and should not be done regardless of some other condition.

However, worms are not the only parasite to attack horses in general and young ones in particular.

In the late winter and early spring, a growing horse can become run down. Added to the demands of growth and keeping warm is the burden of growing a new coat for the summer. Equally, it is said that 'no horse looks well at blackberry time', for it is early autumn when blackberries are on the brambles and the horse is having to grow a winter coat ready for the cold months ahead. So for similar reasons horses can get run down at the end of the summer. If you are unlucky and your horse comes into contact with the eggs or nits of lice, it may become infested with these small creatures. At first, the horse may just appear somewhat scruffy, and then you may notice that the dishevelled appearance is due to rubbing, especially the mane and tail. The hairs get broken, and before long the mane is a stubbly remnant of its former glory. The horse's neck, shoulders and hindquarters could be bald in patches, the remaining coat broken and matted from rubbing. Fortunately, treatment is easy. The horse will need thoroughly dowsing in louse powder. Work it well in with rubber-gloved hands. Two doses should be applied, eleven days apart. The second dose kills any nits that have hatched out since the first crop of lice were destroyed. At first glance, lice look like dandruff, but close inspection reveals their smooth outline. A magnifying glass will show that they are indeed animals as their legs can be seen.

As youngsters will hopefully spend a large part of their youth turned out to grass, they are susceptible to skin diseases such as rain scald, mud fever and cracked heels. These are all caused by the same organism, *Dermatophilus*, and give rise to inflamed, suppurating dermatitis on the back, legs or belly

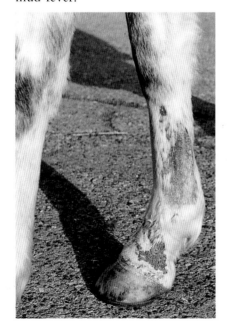

This is a moderately severe case of mud fever.

and heels respectively. It need not rain or be muddy for these conditions to arise — long grass getting wet in the heavy dew can make the skin soft and wet, ideal for the onset of these skin diseases. For this reason, if none other, horses turned away should always be checked carefully for any signs of hot or sore skin, especially on the legs and most particularly where the skin is pink, not pigmented. The horse will need stabling and treating before being turned out again with adequate preventative measures being taken. In muddy conditions, clean dry legs can be protected with a layer of petroleum jelly or zinc and castor oil cream. Lard is an old-fashioned remedy for keeping water or mud off a horse. Also, cod liver oil brushed on to the legs can be effective in keeping mud off and protecting the legs against disease.

Wet mud should not be allowed to dry on to the legs, but should be hosed off with cold water and the clean legs allowed to dry naturally. Rubbing with towels removes the natural greasy protection.

If treatment is necessary, the vet will need to attend and will probably prescribe antibiotics. Cracked heels are especially painful and can cause acute lameness. The angle between the pastern and the heel is usually affected first, then it spreads rapidly up and around the leg. A suitable solvent such as Dermasol is useful as a first step to remove scabs and dried exudate. Once clean, antibiotic can then effectively be applied. Further removal of scabs should not be necessary and is, in any case, painful and upsetting to a young horse. Some cases will clear up in three to six days but others can prove remarkably difficult to clear. Once the scabs turn black, healing usually follows quickly. Treatment should continue until there is no sign of any scabs, soreness or weeping. This author has found comfrey oil to be effective in the treatment of cracked heels. It should be applied daily, over the scabs, until the condition is clear. It has the added benefit of causing the horse little stress in what is an exceptionally painful disease.

In the summer a common problem is photosensitisation, which looks like sunburn and affects pink-skinned areas especially on the muzzle. White legs can also be affected. It is the result of a combination of sunlight and some sensitising

Young horses occasionally get warts, usually on the muzzle. This one has a very extensive crop of warts; in time, her body's defences will make antibodies to the virus causing the warts. The warts will then disappear, never to return.

element in the diet. St John's Wort and perennial ryegrass have been suggested as culprits. It can also be associated with liver disease or malfunction and could be an early indicator of ragwort poisoning. A bad case will need stabling, but it is better to prevent the onset which can be done quite simply by applying sunscreen twice a day. Use a high factor protection (SPE 25) or even total sunblock in a cream formulation suitable for children and preferably unperfumed. Arabs seem particularly susceptible to this annoying condition, which, if untreated, can rapidly become extremely ugly, sore, swollen, scabby and very painful. The affected area can be permanently scarred, forever hypersensitive and hairless.

Just like children, young equines seem to get more than their fair share of coughs and colds. Most are not serious, just requiring a little nursing, protection from cold or wet weather and 'snotty' discharges mopped up frequently. A thin smear of white paraffin or zinc and castor oil cream to cleaned noses will make the next lot of nasal discharge easier to remove or less likely to cause chapping on the muzzle. Do not forget that roundworm will cause cough and cold-like signs; it is also worth bearing in mind that following their first few vaccinations there is the possibility that they might develop very slight flu signs.

Years may pass with no reports of strangles, then there seems to be an explosion of reports of this horrible bacterial infection of the glands in the head and neck. Horses are said not to get this disease twice, so a successful recovery from it must be regarded as beneficial. It can be a killer, in young horses being fatal in from 5 to 20 per cent of cases. Swift action is needed. It is important to isolate the horse and protect it from any adverse weather conditions (including too high a temperature, which can be dehydrating). The horse will appear to have a very sore throat and stand with the head and neck slightly extended. The glands will be obviously swollen. They may or may not form abscesses which burst, discharging blood and pus. So long as these open wounds are kept clean and flies deterred, a swift recovery usually follows. Vets are divided on whether or not to treat with antibiotics, but if a case of strangles is suspected, the vet should always be

Strangles – two-year-old Shetland with heavy nasal discharge.

Two-year-old Shetland with strangles abscess between its lower jaws.

called out. The copious quantities of thick nasal discharge are highly infectious, so the yard must be isolated as well as the horse. It is wise to steam clean and disinfect all stables once the outbreak is over and before other horses come to the yard again.

Obviously there are lots of things horses can get wrong with them. These are just a few of the more common problems with the 'under 4s'. The vet is your ally and must always be called if you are unhappy. It is better to call the vet when it turns out to be nothing than to leave a sick horse to deteriorate. As a general guide, call the vet:

for wounds more than 1 inch through all skin layers;

for marked lameness;

for slight lameness that does not improve in three days;

for any other sign of pain, e.g. colic;

if the horse has a raised temperature (normal is 100.5 °F, or around 38 °C);

if the breathing when rested is rapid or distressed (normal is around 12 breaths per minute);

if the horse has a cough without an obvious cause, such as dusty hay, or fails to stop coughing when dusty hay is removed;

if any minor condition fails to respond to your care in three days;

if you suspect skin parasites;

if you are worried!

18 BITTING

Introducing a young horse to a bit for the first time is usually successful and straightforward. However, if it is not achieved tactfully, quickly and proficiently, second and subsequent occasions may prove less easy.

First, the choice of bit requires some consideration. Traditionally, a so-called mouthing snaffle would have been used. Three keys or players attached to a ring in the centre of the mouthpiece are intended to make the bit more interesting to the youngster and encourage it to mouth on the bit. This creates saliva and reduces the risk of a sore mouth arising, which occurs when pressure is put on the bit while the mouth is dry. Without the lubricating effect of saliva, the bit can chafe. In practice, however, the presence of an unusual object in the mouth causes sufficient interest for the horse to mouth it anyway. It has been found that a mouthing snaffle can in fact serve to annoy the horse, which will possibly end up putting its tongue over the bit in order to avoid the irritation of the keys on its tongue. This is to be discouraged at all costs, because the bit can damage the frenulum, the delicate tissue under the tongue. Also the pressure of the bit on the sensitive bars is more direct and stronger, and the horse can even choke due to the retracted tongue blocking the airway as it attempts to pull the tongue back and over the bit. Once the horse has got the habit of getting the tongue over the bit, it is difficult to correct and may require the use of contraptions in the mouth (tongue grids or tongue layers) to prevent it happening. Racehorses which do this may even have the tongue strapped down to the lower jaw. Such solutions are

(*Opposite*) Lorna and Chieftain ready to take some walking exercise. He wears a rubber bit, but Lorna also leads him from the headcollar fitted with the bridle — the bit is used only if he gets too strong. Note that Lorna wears hat, gloves, a shirt (perhaps long sleeves would be even better) and carries a whip.

best avoided by not allowing the problem to develop in the first place.

At this early stage, for leading the young horse, a straight bit rather than a jointed one is appropriate. A jointed bit can prove too strong in use, with the result that the youngster can become frightened of the nutcracker action on the lower jaws and end up running backwards in fear, away from the pain being inflicted. Use of a metal bit is best avoided, especially now there are modern materials available as satisfactory alternatives. Metal is very hard and can be painful if it accidentally hits a tooth. It is also cold and heavy.

A nylon mouthpiece is a very satisfactory one to use at first. The material is fairly resistant to chewing, is very light, feels warm and is quite resilient so does not need to be too thick. Unlike rubber, it does not taste unpleasant and does not require the horse to open its mouth very wide to admit the bit. It is also less likely to chafe than rubber. It is inflexible, so the horse is not encouraged to become complacent as it gets accustomed to the bit, so is unlikely to develop the habit of leaning on the bit — another annoying habit which will have serious implications as the horse gets older and starts ridden work.

When putting the bit on for the first time, have it fitted to a very simple bridle. If you have an old slip head and cheek from a double bridle (bridoon strap) this will be very satisfactory, or just a headpiece with cheekpieces. The bridle will not be on for long the first time, so the fewer straps to fit or get in the way the better. Line the bridle up with the horse's head to get a reasonable idea of the size required and adjust it accordingly. If in doubt, fit the bit a little on the low side. If it is too high, the bridle could be too tight to get over the horse's ears. Have the keepers on the nearside undone so that the bridle can be adjusted quickly, if necessary, once it is on.

At first, fit the skeletal bridle over a headcollar with its leadrope attached and lying over the horse's neck so that it cannot stand on it, but is available if required. The rope on the headcollar provides a means of control without having to use the bit. The noseband of the headcollar needs to be sufficiently loose to allow the mouth to open to accept the bit.

Kassya is having a bridle fitted for the first time. Note how Fliss's right arm and hand keep the horse's head steady, as well as holding the bridle. The thumb of her left hand (not visible) will make the filly open her mouth by touching her tongue. The fingers, holding the bit, will slip it between the teeth when her mouth is open and the right hand will be lifted so the bit cannot fall out again. The headcollar is left on. The noseband is sufficiently loose to allow the mouth to open. Fliss wears a hard hat in case Kassya takes objection.

Stand on the nearside of the horse, by the neck and facing forwards. Put your right arm under and around the head, and then pass the bridle from your left hand to your right and position it just as you would when bridling an older horse. Line the bit up with the mouth; use the thumb of your left hand in the corner of the mouth to encourage the horse to open it. Tickle its tongue if necessary or apply gentle downwards pressure on the bar. As the mouth opens, slip the bit in with your left hand and pull the headpiece over the horse's right ear with your right hand. Then use both hands to tidy the forelock and tuck the left ear into the bridle. Adjust the height of the bit if necessary.

Do not bridle a horse which is tied up. It could panic and pull back. If it will not stand still, have an assistant hold it by the headcollar. Approach the whole episode with confidence and keep going until you have achieved your goal. Do not be put off, if, for instance, the youngster puts its head up or moves off. Just keep going and do what you set out to do.

(*Opposite*) A collection of bridles for leading youngsters.
From the left:
(1) Rubber snaffle with chain-end lead rein through the rings.
(2) Colt show bridle, stainless steel bit with horseshoe-shaped rings and chain-end lead rein on a coupling.
(3) Bitless in-hand show bridle suitable for a filly; all leather, buckle-end lead rein.
(4) Skeletal bridle (just a slip head or bridoon strap) with a straight nylon bit, coupling and stout rope for leading at home.
(5) Colt show bridle with nylon eggbut ringed snaffle, chain-end lead rein through the rings.

Once the bridle is safely on, gently pat the horse, telling it how good and clever it is. *Do not* feed it as it could find eating difficult and may try to put the tongue over the bit.

At first it is not easy to see if the bit is at the correct height, for the youngster will probably mouth the bit actively, but after a few minutes will settle down and it is possible to check more closely. The bit should be fitted sufficiently high to make it almost impossible to get the tongue over, but not so high as to stretch the lips into a weird kind of grin! The corners of the mouth will be slightly wrinkled. So long as the bit is at least wide enough not to pinch at the sides, it does not matter at first if it is too wide, but for leading and showing, the correct width of bit is needed. There should be about ¼ inch (5 mm) between the bit rings and the corner of the horse's mouth. Bits are measured in a straight line between the rings, and range in size from 4 to 6 inches to fit all sized horses from Shetland ponies to a Shire. Most riding horses take a 5 or 5½ inch bit.

Do not leave the horse alone with the bridle on. After a few minutes take it off again, in effect reversing the procedure to put it on. Put your right arm under the head and hold the head steady. Slip out the left ear and then the right and gently lower the bridle. As the horse feels the bit descend in the mouth it will usually spit it out, but if it seems reluctant to let go, hold the bridle with your right hand and gently open the mouth with your left hand. Make quite sure you do not bang the teeth nor allow the horse to throw up its head.

Once the youngster has had a chance to get used to the bit, it can be fitted on to a full bridle or an in-hand show bridle and then it can be taught to lead from the bit. Use a three way coupling which also links on to the noseband, or use a second leadrope on the noseband. This avoids the need to put excessive pressure on the mouth too soon. Always use a coupling. This is a device that buckles on to the two bit rings (and the noseband too, if a three-way coupling) and the lead rein is then attached to the coupling. A lead rein threaded through one bit ring and fastened to the other can be very severe as it can tighten under the jaw, so is not to be recommended.

Use the bit only as an aid to improve control. Never use it as a means of punishment.

Encourage the horse to walk forward confidently and gradually to accept a light contact with your hand through the lead rein and the bit. Do not leave the horse alone in the stable bitted. It could get caught and cause an accident or the horse could become bored with it and start trying to find a way to resist it, such as putting its tongue back or holding the bit between the back teeth. All these will result in further problems once schooling for ridden work starts later on.

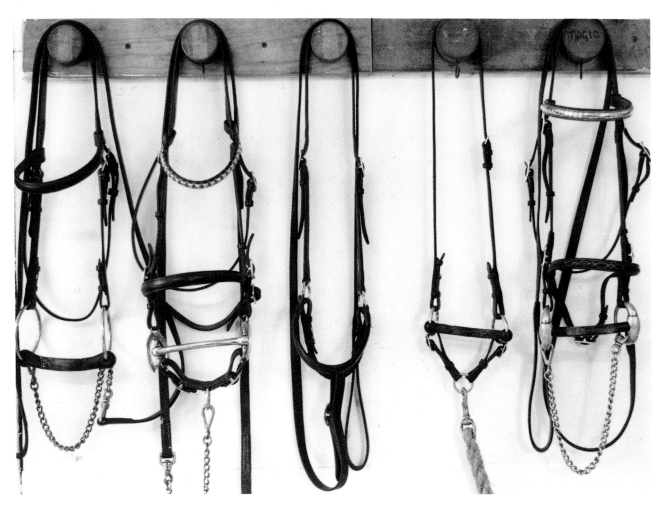

19 CONCLUSION

Horses have been evolving for 55 million years, but have been domesticated for only, at the most, five thousand years. During that short space of time, man has fashioned the horse to suit his needs, working in a compromise with nature. The horse has been developed in different areas to perform the various tasks required of it, but until very recently has existed in a semi-wild or feral state. These more or less free-living herds acted as a self-perpetuating reservoir from which man helped himself as and when required.

Gradually, this system has been refined and now most horses are kept in a far more organised manner, on restricted areas and frequently stabled. Horses are amazingly adaptable and many will tolerate a life style of individual confinement in a stable, even up to twenty-four hours a day. But it should never be forgotten how far it is from the natural state, of roaming in sociable herds on open, grassland plains. Whilst an older horse may have become habituated to its unnatural existence, a young horse is going through a sometimes traumatic process to achieve acceptance of its very different lot. The instincts and urges of 55 million years of evolution will be stronger than the influence of even five thousand years of domestication. In fact, so powerful are the wild instincts of horses that domesticated horses turned loose and free of human influence will return to a wild herd structure, similar to that of plains-dwelling zebra, within five years.

Domestication for the horse is a deal with man. In return for the horse's compliance with our needs or wishes, we have saved the species from extinction. There are probably no free-

(*Opposite*) Young Thoroughbreds around a safe, sophisticated type of water trough.

173

living, truly wild horses left in the world, although there are many successful feral herds bearing testimony to the innate wildness in all horses.

A young horse must learn to accept the conditions and restraints of domesticity. Its early growing years assume a much greater importance in this context, and are very influential in how it will later accept the additional restraints of working for its human gaoler.

With tact, sympathy, understanding and firmness, it is possible to ease the young horse's transition from innately wild to fully domesticated. Once its baser, instinctive drives and urges are understood, it is possible to co-operate with them rather than fight against them in order to achieve the desired result in training. Brute force may eventually persuade a horse to go somewhere it would prefer not; how much better if it learns to go there with no fight, no fear, no argument, by following a trusted companion. How much better that it socialise in an interesting field with at least one other 'herd member' than learn to weave as its distress in confinement finally trips it over the edge of sanity.

It is my hope that this book will help the reader prepare the young horse in his or her care for its adult life by knowing what a horse requires and by understanding where the horse came from, before taking it somewhere profoundly alien and creating problems which will remain for ever.

That most horses can apparently quite happily accept the life style imposed upon them by humans is a miracle. That some do not, and develop behavioural problems, is only to be expected. So far from their roots, all horses deserve a great deal of respect, and probably far more understanding than most of them get.

My wish is that readers will gain a fraction of the pleasure from their young horses that I have had from mine, and that theirs will become better adult horses as a result of their owner's heightened understanding of them.

Tailpiece.

INDEX

Page numbers in *italics* refer to illustrations

acorns *59*
aerosols 60–1
ailments 157–65
amino acids 105, 106
approaching foal 21, 25–6

bandages 119, 152–3
barley 107
  grass 138
bits 168, 170
  colts 150–1
bitting 167–71
black nightshade *44*, 45
blind spots 24–5
bots 131–2
bran 109
bridle 119, 123, 168–70
broom *46*
brushes 29, 34
buckets 19, 20, 55
buttercups 45, 51–2
buying 3

calcium 92, 107, 109
cannon, offset 90
canter 80
carotene 77, 111
carriage horses 82
carrots 111
castration 134–6

catching 21–7, 55
cavesson 119, 123
chaff *see* chop
challenges 149
change 145–6
chewing 102
chop 109
cleaning 13–14
coat 58, *61*, 62, 77
  diet 77, 113
  winter *61*, 62, 75, 77
cold hosing 159–60
colds 164
colts 134–5, 150–1
companions 15, 16–17, 26, 38, 98
  development of young horse
    39–40
  loading 120, 123
  necessity 40–1
concentrates 105–6, 110–11, 114
copper deficiency 54
coughs 164
cow parsley *44*
crib-biting 18
curbs 90–1

day length 77
delivery 7
Dermatophilus 162–3
developmental problems 98–9

diet
  coat changing 77
  epiphysitis 92
  high-grade 103
  leg problems 91
  navicular disease 96
  supplements 113
  see also feeding
dishing 89–90
ditches 51, 147, *148*
domestication 173–4
door fastenings 20
doorway 14–15, 146
drainage 51
drains 13
driving 124
droppings *48*, 49
  eating 108, 109
  worm egg count 132

electrical fittings 18–19
emasculator 135
epiphyseal closure *93*
epiphysitis 92

farriery 132–4
feeding 55, 101–14
  eating time 102, 103
  from the hand 27, 55
  habits 102

quantity 113—14
see also diet
feet 34—5, 49, 89, 132
  branding 57
  navicular disease 95—6
fertilisers 53
floors 13
fly repellants 59—60
fomenting 160—1
freeze-branding 56—7

garlic 96
gelding *see* castration
grain 107, 108
grass 48, 49, 50, 51, 105
  young horse at 55—63, 98
  see also pasture management
grazing 43, 111, 130
grooming 29, 34—6, 77
  tying up 65—6
growth 37, 38, 89—99
  limbs 94
  nutritional requirements 103
  uneven 58—9, 92—3
  yearling 58—9, 61

habits, bad 17—18
hard feed *see* concentrates
harrowing *48*, 49, 53, 130
hay 53, 62, 102, *104*, *112*, 114
  for travelling 7, 117, 126
haylage 117
haynet 7
head, yearling 96—7
headcollar 22, *28*, 118, 119
hemlock *44*, 45
herd behaviour 101
hernia 91—2
hocks 91, *92*
hooves 84
  see also feet
Horse of the Year Show 77—8
horsebox 115
housing 11, 12

incisors 139, 141
influenza vaccination 127
injuries 60—1, 157, 158
itchiness 29—30

joints, clicking 94
judge 70, 71, 72, 73

kicking 17, 23, 24, 25, 34, 72
  boards 13
knee
  open 92
  splints 90
knots 31

laburnum 45, *46*
laminitis 53, 109
leading 23—4, 26
  distance from handler 66—8
  showing 78—9
  two year olds 66—8
learning 145—54
leaving alone 15
legs
  crooked 89, 90
  dietary problems 91
  growth 94
  injury 152
  mud 163
  post 94
lice 162
liming 52, 53
loading 118—20, *121—2*, 123—4
lucerne 106, 109
lunge lines/rein 23—4, 119
lungworm 130
lysine 107

mane plaiting 75, 83—4
manure 53—4
microchip insertion 57
milk pellets/powder 110
molars 139, 141, 142
monkey mouth 140
mouthing snaffle 167

muzzle hairs 25

navicular disease 94—6
nettles 48
noise 146

oats 107
oestrus 97
organophosphorus compounds
  131—2
osteochondrosis 94

paddocks 43
paint 14
parrot mouth 139—40
pasture management 43—54
  drainage 51
  fertilisers 53
  harrowing *48*, 49, 53, 130
  liming 52, 53
  reseeding 50—1
  resting 132
  soil quality 51—2
  topping 45, 47—8
  weeds 43—4
  worms 130
pedigree 4
photographs 57
photosensitisation 163—4
plaiting 75, 83—4
play 98
poaching 50, 65
poisonous plants *44*, 45—6, 47, 48,
  59, 105
poulticing 160
privet *46*
protein 105, 106

quidding 137—8

ragwort *44*, 45, 105
records 58
redworm *104*, 129, 130
registration 4, 85
releasing 26—7

reseeding 50
rewards 27, 55, 82
rhinopneumonitis 127
roots 111
ropes 23–4, 26, *28*, 30, 33–4
    clips 33, *34*, 118
roundworms 128, 130
rugs 62, 75, 77, 117

salt lick, mineralised 108
seaweed, calcified 52–3
security 55–8
sewage sludge 53
shelter 11, 12, 59, 62, 65
shoes 132–3
showing 68, 69–88
    breed classes 74, 81, 82–3, 85
    entries 87–8
    handler's turnout 84–5
    height 87
    judge 70, 71, 72, 73, 86
    leading 78–9
    overweight horses 69–70
    paces 72–3, 79–81
    paperwork 85–8
    plaiting 75, 83–4
    preparation 75, 83
    procedure 70–4
    show types 85–6
    standing 81–3
    stewards 71
    training 74, 75
    travelling 74
slot seeding 50
soil 51–2
soundness 89, 154
splints 90
stable muck 53
stabling 11, 12, 15, 40
standing 81–3, 134
stimulation 147–9

stomach hair worm 130
strangles 164–5
stride 72–3
studs 3, 5
suckling 16
sugar beet pulp 107–8, 109, 131

tail plaiting/pulling 75, 84
tapeworm 49, 129, 131
teeth 96–7, 137–43
    milk 139, *140*, 141, 142, 143
    misalignment 139–40
    permanent 139, *140*, 141
    rasping 137, 138, 139
teething 142–3
testosterone 134–5
tetanus vaccination 127
theft 55–6
tie ring *28*, 30, 32, 33
    vehicle 117–18
tie up 6, 27, *28*, 29, 30–4
    grooming 65–6
toes, turning in/out 89–90
topping 51
trailer 115, 118
travelling 6–9, 115–26
    breaks in journey 125, 126
    companion 120, 123, 126
    direction of horse 125–6
    driving 124
    hay 117, 126
    loading 118–20, *121–2*, 123–4
    rugs 117
    tying up 117–18
    unloading 123, 125
    vehicle 115
trotting 79–80
tubbing 161
turf 49, 50
tush 142
two year olds 65–8, 88

vaccination 49, 87, 127
vegetable oil 113
vehicle
    cladding 116
    floor 116
    partitions 115–16
    tie rings 117–18
    ventilation 116
    windows 116
vetting 5, 154
vices 17–18
vision 24, 119
vitamin A 77, 111
vitamin D 113

walking 68, 79, 149–52
water supply 19, 20
weaning 5, 16, 17
weather, protection from 11–12,
    59, 62, 65
weaving 14, 18, 102
weeds 43–4
wind-sucking 18
wintering out 62–3, 65
wolf teeth 139
woody nightshade *44*, 45
workload 153–4
worming 127–32, 162
worms 43, 49, 104, 130, 132, 162
wounds
    cold hosing 159–60
    fomenting 160–1
    healing 157–8
    poulticing 160
    tubbing 161

yards 11
yearling 37–8, 88, 89
    at grass 37–8, 55–63
    head 96–7
yew 45–6